From This Day Forward

The marriage of writer Madeleine L'Engle and actor Hugh
Franklin was one of lasting love, a true union of mind and
spirit. It was a long-term marriage of over forty years
between two gifted people, 'full of wonderful things,
terrible things, joyous things, grievous things – but ours'.

Together they faced the problem of two separate careers.
Together they struggled to maintain the priority of family
life. Together they faced success and failure.

When they first met, Hugh Franklin was an established
actor, Madeleine L'Engle a small-part actress at the start of
her writing career. She tells the story of their courtship, of
Crosswicks, the old Connecticut farmhouse which provided
the warm centre and heart of family life – the story of their
meeting, their life together – and of their parting.

The tragic news of Hugh's illness from cancer comes
early in the narrative. And gradually the story focuses on
the parting. This is an honest and open account of their
hopes and fears, a tribute to lifelong love and enduring
faith.

After her first successful novels MADELEINE L'ENGLE
accumulated a vast number of rejection slips before her
seventh book, *A Wrinkle in Time*, won the Newbery Prize,
the highest award for children's fiction in the United States.
Since then she has written more than thirty books for both
adults and children and several volumes of poetry. She and
her husband brought up three children. Madeleine
continues to travel and lecture extensively.

FOR HUGH

FROM THIS DAY FORWARD

MADELEINE L'ENGLE

A LION PAPERBACK
Oxford · Batavia · Sydney

Copyright © 1988 Crosswicks Ltd

Published by
Lion Publishing plc
Sandy Lane West, Littlemore, Oxford, England
ISBN 0 7459 1802 6
Albatross Books Pty Ltd
PO Box 320, Sutherland, NSW 2232, Australia
ISBN 0 7324 0151 8

First British edition 1989

Printed in Great Britain
by Cox and Wyman Ltd, Reading

I

PRELUDE

One

---

*C*rosswicks is a typical New England farmhouse, built some-
time in the middle of the eighteenth century, so it is well over
two hundred years old. Its square central section has been added
to haphazardly over the years, white clapboard somehow tying
it all together, so that the house rambles pleasantly and crookedly.
A dropped ball will roll right to the central chimneys, and the
bookcases we've built in are masterpieces of non-alignment.

Crosswicks is a symbol for me of family and community life,
of marriage in general and my own marriage in particular. It
stands staunchly on the crest of one of the Litchfield hills in the
northwest corner of Connecticut and through the centuries has
withstood the batterings of many storms—blizzards, hurricanes,
even a tornado—of love, anger, birth, death, tears, laughter.

Perhaps it is a particularly potent symbol for me because, until
the house came to us over forty years ago, I had never lived in
a real house, much less had one of my own. I was born on the
asphalt island of Manhattan and lived for my first twelve years
in an apartment. I had my own small back bedroom, its one
window looking onto a court, where the stories of other city
dwellers were sometimes enacted for me behind unshaded win-

dows or on the rooftop of a building lower than ours. I was an only child, with an ailing father, and lived a solitary life. My parents had dinner at eight o'clock in the evening, and I had my meal on a tray in my room and ate happily, with my feet on the desk and a book on my chest.

It was a totally different childhood from that of my husband, Hugh Franklin, who had a much more typically American upbringing, growing up in Tulsa, Oklahoma, in a comfortable, unpretentious house on a pleasant, tree-lined street of similar houses filled with professional father, stay-at-home mother, and many other children on the block to play with.

How different were Hugh's and my early years; each of us was given different treasures, different sorrows. I grew up in a world of books, music, theatre, a small world where the artist was the norm, rather than the odd one out.

Hugh grew up in a world where artists were thought to belong to a half-world of permissiveness and promiscuity. His father was a distinguished lawyer, and there were books in the house, though not many, according to the standards of my parents. The First Baptist Church was central. Regular churchgoing was compulsory. To be a "Christian" was essential.

My mother and father were Episcopalians, but being a "Christian" was secondary (if it was thought about at all) to being a good and faithful singer, or painter, or writer.

Totally different worlds.

My father was a writer, a journalist and foreign correspondent and news analyst, though mustard gas in the trenches of World War I stopped much of his traveling. My parents' friends were painters, sculptors, singers, actors, composers. The world of the nineteen-twenties seemed a world of parties. A terrible war had ended. People played almost frantically. Mother and Father were either dressing to go out to a party or the theatre or the opera or they were preparing to have friends come in.

I was on the fringe of that world, a child isolated in my own room, but aware of and taking for granted the music, the laughter, the conversation going on in the rest of the apartment.

My parents had been married for nearly twenty years when I was born, and although I was a very much wanted baby, the pattern of their lives was already well established and a child was not part of that pattern. So I had my own, with which I was well content, reading and rereading, writing stories and poems; illustrating my stories with pencil and watercolors; playing the piano; living far too much in an interior dream world. But that interior dream world has stood me in good stead many times when the outer world has seemed to be collapsing around me.

After my childhood in New York came a time of wandering about Europe, trying to find air clean and pure enough for my father's damaged lungs. World War I, which had little place in Hugh's early life, remained paramount in mine, along with the fear of war.

What I, overprotected by my solitude rather than my parents' design, did not realize was that the terrible Wall Street crash of '29 had affected everyone's lives. More imminent was the fact that my father was in the hospital with pneumonia, that my mother could not hide that she was frantic with anxiety. Then the crisis was over and he was home, but nothing was the same.

We were moving, leaving New York and moving to Europe. The doctors had recommended a sanatorium in Saranac, but after the crash, with its consequent Depression, my parents could not afford Saranac. The standard of living in the French Alps, where the air was clean and clear, was much lower than the standard of living in the United States. The Depression had closed down most of the great resort hotels. There were no "beautiful people" and the world was a war away from the jet set. Most of the available *pensions* around the emptied resort hotels had no indoor plumbing and no running water. But the air was the clean, dry air the doctor had recommended. If we stayed in New York my father would be prone to another attack of pneumonia, which might well be lethal. We had to move away from everything I had known.

How my parents must have missed the opera, the theatre, the parties that had been so much a part of their lives in New York. But they shielded me in their Olympian way from feelings which must have bordered on desolation.

Our first home after we sailed from New York was, strangely enough, a château. My parents were planning to have the summer in the French Alps with another family, also devastated by the crash. Mother told me later that the real-estate agent resisted even showing them the château, it was in such terrible condition, but they insisted, and fell in love with its ancient charm. And it was cheap—cheap because nothing much had been done to it since the eleventh century. Well, there was an ancient, pull-chain water closet, but I remember the water for the day being brought to the bedrooms in big china pitchers which had matching wash-bowls. There was a strange bathroom with an enormous bathtub set in a mahogany base. Under the tub was a firebox by which the water was heated. Of course, the firebox made the tub too hot to sit in, so we used it only for occasional cold baths.

Two young women from the village helped out, accustomed to cooking with no running water, no refrigerator, nor, for that matter, a stove. There was a fireplace with a spit suitable for roasting an ox. It is impossible for me to understand what total dislocation this must have represented for my parents. They had not been rich, but they had been surrounded and nourished by the richness of New York's artistic community. Suddenly to be totally uprooted and set down in a tiny provincial village without even a radio for music must have been shocking.

I spent the summer dreaming and wandering through the dusty rooms of the château. The great day for the grownups was Friday, when the horse-drawn fish cart clattered across the cobblestone streets of the village. Not only would there be fish for dinner, but the fish were kept fresh on ice, and my parents were given enough ice so that on Friday evenings they had dry martinis before dinner.

  Meanwhile, in Tulsa, Oklahoma, my as-yet-undreamed-of husband was experiencing the Depression in a very different way. His lawyer father was counsel for one of the big oil companies. Like many others in those plush days before the crash, he had been buying stocks on the margin, for himself, and for friends. The Franklin family lived comfortably, and Hugh's older brother and sister were sent to college. Hugh, much younger, was still at home, about to enter high school, when the crash came. His father lost everything. Unlike some businessmen, he did not jump out his office window or declare bankruptcy. Instead, he spent the next quarter of a century working, and at the time of Hugh's and my marriage in 1946 he had just finished paying back to his friends and acquaintances every penny he had lost in investing for them in the stock market. A man of great integrity and honor.

But while Hugh was growing up, there was no money. Only a summer ago Hugh told of his humiliation in going to the junior prom in a brown suit. He was the only boy in his large class at

Tulsa Central High who could not afford to rent a tuxedo. The girl he was taking to the prom made excuses to leave early. After all these years, the memory still caused him deep pain.

• Certainly, no adolescence is lived through without pain. •

The summer of the château, my twelfth summer, came to an end and I was sent to my first boarding school, this one in Switzerland. My parents moved through a succession of rented villas, *pensions*, and small hotels. My father's lungs did not improve; my mother's health was delicate. During school holidays I stayed with them wherever they were, and it was their presence, rather than place, which gave me a sense of home.

The closest we came to living in a house was when we returned to the United States and, after my grandmother's death, went to live in her beach cottage, perched atop a dune in north Florida. I adored it, although I was never there for more than a few weeks at a time. In the summer I was sent off to camp; in the winter I was in boarding school, Ashley Hall, in Charleston, South Carolina. My parents were not trying to "get rid" of me. I knew that they unqualifiedly loved me. But life was hard enough for them without the added needs of a lonely teenager. And they were trying to protect me from their own pain. My father was dying. My mother was emotionally and physically drained.

We all loved the old beachhouse. It was built for summer, with the house open, back and front, to the breeze, and with a wide veranda wrapped all the way around to provide shade. In the winter it was bitter cold. North Florida is not like Miami or Palm Beach. It has the beautiful and ancient trees that south Florida does not have—the water oaks, the live oaks, the camphor trees, the tall pines. It also has a raw northeast wind, and my parents (and I, during the holidays) wore layers of clothes as though we were at a ski resort. But there was always the beauty of the ocean, with the wide white beach in front of the house, with the lagoon and jungle behind. And I had my own room, my first real room to myself since leaving New York. I had an old cherrywood desk that had belonged to my great-grandmother Madeleine L'Engle, and mahogany bookcases with sliding glass fronts which protected the books at least a little from the damp.

My father finally died from pneumonia when I was seventeen, the autumn of my last year in boarding school. My mother sold the house at the beach—I was too full of grief even to weep, or to understand that she had no choice. When I went home for Christmas, it was to an apartment in Jacksonville. My mother was to live there the rest of her long life. The great blessing of the apartment was the view of the St. Johns River—St. Johns Bay, it was called when she was young. The river curved about the spit of land on which the apartment was built, and she could see the sun both rise and set over the water.

I graduated from Ashley Hall and went on to Smith College, with my mother never for a second making me feel that I "ought" to give up my own life and take care of her. She was a woman remarkably capable of taking care of herself.

ᴥ Hugh grew up on one street in one house—the same house where his sister and brother-in-law now live.

One December we had the amazing experience of going to their golden wedding celebration in the house where their parents had had their golden wedding anniversary on a street that has not changed. Extraordinary, in this day and age.

Hugh's brother-in-law has completely renovated the house and it is beautiful and comfortable. But when Hugh was growing up, there was no money for anything but the barest essentials, and he was able to go to college only because he won a full scholarship to Northwestern University's famous School of Speech. Though he couldn't afford to rent that tux for the high school prom, he was president of the Honor Society, had leads in all the school plays, and by his junior year had been picked out by a talent scout for Northwestern.

Tulsa was a "one-night stand" for touring theatrical companies, and one evening Hugh was taken to see the legendary Walter Hampden in *Cyrano de Bergerac*. From that evening on, acting was not just an extracurricular high school activity; it was his life.

❧ My own high school and college years were a mixture of joy and pain. I loved Ashley Hall, where for the first time I was happy in school. In the lower grades I was a non-achiever. At Ashley Hall I found my stride and was appreciated and a leader— except at the school dances. Most of the Southern boys who went to those dances were considerably shorter than I. There is nothing more mortifying than having your partner's head below your neck. But these school dances came only once or twice a year. Far worse were the debut parties I had to attend during the holidays when I took the train down to Florida. I was the outsider in a closely knit group of young people who had grown up together in Jacksonville, gone to school together, would marry one another. Because my mother had been born and reared in this Southern city, I was invited to the dances and coming-out parties and dates were arranged for me. "Arranged" is right. I don't think I ever had a young man call me on his own in Jacksonville until I was ready to graduate from college. There may be something to be said for arranged marriages; there is little to say for arranged dates.

Seafood was frequently served at the dinner parties, and I assumed that the reason I often had to excuse myself and hurry to the bathroom to throw up was my inadequacy as a social butterfly. I did not know how to make small talk, and large talk was discouraged. Despite lessons, I was clumsy on the dance floor. I stepped on my partner's toes or tripped over my own feet. I hated every minute of these debutante parties and threw up a good many dinners. Years later I discovered that I am allergic to bivalves, to the very oysters, clams, and scallops that were so popular. The combination of the double allergy was abysmal. I couldn't wait to go back to school.

When I graduated from college and started to work in the theatre, I was able to manage my visits South at times other than the debutante season. I am grateful that Hugh and I didn't meet until we had both learned at least a little more about other people and about ourselves than we knew during those early years of painful growth.

Two

After college I headed like a homing pigeon for New York. It was the place of my birth. It was where I would find music and art, theatre and publishing; it was where I belonged.

When I came to New York in the early autumn of 1941, the glamorous world my parents had known during the twenties had long been gone. We were heading toward the destruction of Pearl Harbor and the entrance of the United States into World War II. The rest of my known world was already at war. For me that war had started when I was still at Ashley Hall and heard that Mussolini had marched his troops into Ethiopia. I still remember my stark feeling of terror as I realized that yet another ghastly war could not be averted.

But ordinary life kept on. My college roommate and I found an apartment on Ninth Street in Greenwich Village. In order to cut expenses, we shared it with several other aspiring young artists. A few blocks away, Hugh was living in an equally crowded apartment, and was beginning to get roles on Broadway. But we were not to meet for several years more.

I provided the furniture for the Ninth Street apartment, cherishing the few pieces my parents had not given away but had put into storage. There was only one bed, a lovely French mahogany bed with the wood curved into swans' necks. We bought a double-decker bed, and a sofa bed for the living room. My mother loved the apartment; it was for her a reminder of the old happy days, and she helped us decorate it. The little room with the French mahogany bed was hers, and though we sometimes let a temporary roommate use it, it was vacated and cleaned whenever Mother came.

My greatest treasure in the apartment was my mother's piano, the parlor grand on which I had practiced as a child and around which so many of my parents' parties were held. One of our roommates came because of the piano. She was a budding musician and filled the apartment with Beethoven, Brahms, and Bach, though after she came I played only when she wasn't around. She grew as she played, not only in technique but in maturity. The great masters pushed her as she tried faithfully to go where they led. We do learn and develop when we are exposed to those who are greater than we are. Perhaps this is the chief way we mature.

Barrels of china and glass came to me from the storage house, and I unpacked them with reverence, pulling each piece out of the sawdust and feeling a marvelous sense of continuity. My mother was not with us for this; it would probably have been too painful for her, a poignant reminder of a life gone forever.

When we distributed the household jobs I announced that I would do the cooking. And that is how I learned to cook—by doing it, and discovering that I was good at it. During my early childhood there had been trips to Europe before our move from New York when I was twelve. So I was a little more experimental about food than many of my contemporaries. I remembered one summer in Brittany when I would be sent off for the day to explore, carrying my lunch of sour bread, sweet butter, and bitter chocolate. This taught me to mix taste and texture. I felt that one does not cook with water, so I learned to keep stocks and juices in the fridge. Cooking was definitely a creative act.

As we settled into the apartment I had visions of work in the theatre, of books published, of romantic love, which had little to do with real love. I wrote stories, which I sent out to little magazines and university quarterlies. And of course I was working on my first novel.

But I needed to earn money, and such small literary magazines pay only in prestige. The theatre beckoned. What wonderful hours for a writer! And Equity minimum was sixty-five dollars a week. In the decade of the forties, Broadway was the Great White Way; stars were brilliant with talent. American musicals came into their own with the production of *Oklahoma!* Serious plays could run without loss for several months, slowly building an audience.

But how could I fit into such a world? True, I had been a success as an actress in school and college. One of my best roles in high school was Sir Andrew Aguecheek in *Twelfth Night*. In a girls' school those of us who were tallest played the male roles. In college I was finally able to play women. But the professional theatre? Broadway?

It so happened that the year of my return to New York was also the year that Eva Le Gallienne, Margaret Webster, and Joseph Schildkraut were offering free auditions to any young theatrical aspirant who wanted to apply. Eva Le Gallienne and Joseph Schildkraut were starring in a Broadway play, *Uncle Harry*. Margaret Webster had brilliantly staged an innovative production of *Othello*, with singer Paul Robeson in the title role.

There were giants in the theatre in those days. Eva Le Gallienne was the founder of the Civic Repertory Theatre. She was a star when she was only fourteen years old and played opposite Joseph Schildkraut in Ferenc Molnár's *Liliom*. Schildkraut—Pepé, as he was known to his friends—was a dashing young Austrian actor, son of the famous Rudolph Schildkraut. In the still occasionally rerun Cecil De Mille film *The King of Kings*, Rudolph played Caiaphas, and Pepé played Judas. His last role on Broadway was the father in *The Diary of Anne Frank*. This was also the first role my husband played on his return to the theatre, after nearly a decade of living year-round at Crosswicks while we raised our children and nurtured our marriage.

Margaret Webster, like Joseph Schildkraut, came of a theatrical family. Her father was the actor Ben Franklin; her mother, Dame May Whitty, whom I had loved in Hitchcock's *The Lady Vanishes*. Peggy Webster was a fine actress, playing Emilia in *Othello*, but she was best known as a director, particularly of Shakespeare's plays, though she was also called on to stage some of the operas at the Metropolitan.

Those three, Le Gallienne, Schildkraut, Webster, were part of a galaxy of stars including Katharine Hepburn, Judith Anderson, John Gielgud, Maurice Evans, Helen Hayes, Alfred Lunt, Lynn Fontanne, with all of whom Hugh was ultimately to play. Many of these "greats" had a soft spot for the young and starstruck and saw to it that the seats in the back row of the top balcony of the theatre often sold for one dollar.

Another opportunity for theatregoing was given us by the American Theatre Wing, which organized the sale of war bonds in theatre lobbies. When the curtain came up and the lobby emptied, we were allowed to go into the theatre and stand in the back and watch the play, or slip into an unoccupied seat. Those who were lazy and did not sell many bonds were sent night after night to *Angel Street*, a popular and long-running Victorian thriller which was fun the first few nights one saw it but did not wear well.

Amazingly, I was successful in selling the bonds, so I was sent from theatre to theatre and ultimately saw everything on Broadway. My method was to approach middle-aged men, smile shyly, and hopefully ask them to buy. What I had going for me was youth and earnestness. I was no great beauty, being overtall (though my long legs were probably more help than I realized) and awkward; my shyness was not feigned. But something worked, and I had an excellent record of sales and a wonderful opportunity to see plays, musicals, whatever was going on in the theatres around the Great White Way. And I learned, subconsciously probably more than consciously, about acting and writing.

And I sent in my application for an audition to Miss Le Gallienne, Mr. Schildkraut, and Miss Webster, and waited for my turn. They were, of course, deluged with applications, but my appointment was scheduled for early in the winter.

Somehow or other I had the sense to choose material that was very different from what most of the other girls were doing. Scenes from Shakespeare and Chekhov abounded. I made up a short monologue from Katherine Mansfield's letters, chose a dramatic scene from an almost unknown play of Molnár's. My two roles were just right for a tall, gawky, myopic young woman. When I got up onstage and started speaking, suddenly these three generous stars heard something completely different from the traditional Juliets and Ninas and Lady Macbeths with which they'd been inundated. They listened. At the end of my allotted time I left the stage. I had brought with me the manuscript of a play I had just written, and with both timidity and audacity handed it to Miss Webster and fled.

A few days later my phone rang. The understudy was leaving *Uncle Harry* and I was offered her job.

❧ And so I was on Broadway. As well as understudying the women's roles, I had a small part as matron of a prison in the last scene, and two lines: "But it might be important, sir." "But it can't do any harm." I wore a long, dark Victorian dress, powdered my hair, and added two greying braids to make me look old, though I suspect I looked very young and clumsy anyhow.

Miss Le Gallienne was deluged with mail, and suggested that I supplement my Equity minimum salary by helping her. So most evenings I spent sitting in her dressing room answering letters. I didn't learn anything unusual from this job, since she kept the more interesting letters for herself and I was given the run-of-the-mill fan ones. But I did learn a great deal about the theatre and about acting and about artistic intuition, not only from the stories she told me about her life and her development as an actress, but even more from her response to each evening's performance.

Perhaps the most important thing I learned is that the artist is not separate from the work and therefore cannot judge it. Some nights Miss Le Gallienne would come drooping back to the dressing room. "I gave a terrible performance this evening. I couldn't get the audience to respond to a thing." Almost invariably when people came backstage after such a declaration, an old friend would cry out enthusiastically, "Eva, that was the best performance I've ever seen you give. You were superb."

On other evenings she would come bounding in. "Oh, it went well tonight! I had them eating out of the palm of my hand!" Almost invariably Thelma, the stage manager, who was also an old friend from the Civic Repertory days, would knock on the door, poke her head in, and ask anxiously, "LeG, are you all right?"

We do not know and cannot tell when the spirit is with us. Great talent or small, it makes no difference. We are caught within our own skins, our own sensibilities; we never know if our technique has been adequate to the vision. Without doubt this is true of my own work, too. I never know, when I have finished a book, how much of what has been in my mind and heart has come through my fingers and onto the page. This inability truly to assess one's own accomplishment is what makes rejections so bitter. When I was receiving rejections from publisher after publisher, I wondered sadly if the book I had conceived in my mind had failed utterly in getting onto the page. This lack of knowing makes the artist terribly vulnerable. When I hand in a manuscript to agent or editor I am filled with anxiety until I hear: Yes, the book is there. It needs work, but it is there.

⨎ When *Uncle Harry* closed for the summer—we were going on tour in the autumn—I was ready to move from the Ninth Street apartment, much as I had loved it, and much as I had learned from communal living. But cooking for our gang, usually eight or more people, was time-consuming. There were too many distractions, and I needed time alone. I needed my piano back. I needed uninterrupted time to write.

When I left Ninth Street I was still as naïve and ignorant as a young woman coming to the big city could possibly be. It wasn't that I was a country cousin; the city was mine; it was my home town. But I knew nothing of its lures or its dangers, and it was to some extent my innocence that protected me.

I found my own small walk-up on Twelfth Street. I began to move outside the circle of friends from the Ninth Street apartment. One of my few friends from Florida, Pat, was in New York at the other end of the city, up at Columbia, where she was an instructor and was taking essential pre-med courses she had missed in college. Pat was, is, as tall as I am, excited by the same beauties, equally inept with small talk. Our idea of joy when we were in Florida was to borrow her school canoe and spend the day paddling the dark backwaters, or to walk for hours in silence on the beach. It was good to have a friend in New York who was as motivated as I was but who was not involved in the strange world of the theatre.

We were (and still are) able to talk about absolutely anything, intimate problems and thoughts one shares with almost nobody. Pat was preparing to enter medical school. I wrote. Got out of bed in the morning and wrote, forgetting breakfast.

Of the Ninth Street group I continued to see Cavada, who did the pots and pans (and still, when she comes to visit, takes over that job despite her elegant clothes and beautifully manicured nails). On occasion I continued to do letters or errands for Miss Le Gallienne, but I spent a lot of time on my own, and began to learn how woefully ignorant I was. My first twelve years in New York I was a nursery child, though my nursery was no more than my own small back bedroom. But I never stopped to wonder how beds got made or tubs got cleaned.

In boarding school I learned to make my bed, but everything else continued to be magically accomplished. During college the making of beds and the moderate tidying of the room was the extent of my housekeeping. Even in the Ninth Street apartment where I became an instant cook, all the rest of the jobs were taken care of by others. It was not until I was living on my own in the walk-up on Twelfth Street that I discovered that sinks and tubs do not stay clean without regular scrubbing. Floors have to be swept and vacuumed, furniture dusted and polished. If I was naïve about housekeeping, I was equally naïve about life.

But at last I was free to experiment, and surely experiment and experience come from the same root.

For ten years, in boarding school and in college, I had been bounded by rules. Times to rise, times to go to bed. Colleges were less free before the Second World War than they are now. We had a curfew: we had to be back in the house by ten o'clock. In New York my friends and I quickly put ourselves on theatre hours. We could go anyplace we wanted at any time we wanted, see whom we wanted where we wanted. Heaven knows it was time for me to be on my own, to live my own life, but my lack of experience caused me to do some incredibly stupid things.

One day shortly before the cast of *Uncle Harry* gathered together for rehearsals to prepare for the tour, Miss Le Gallienne sent me to one of the casting offices. In those days young (and not so young) actors and actresses "made the rounds," going from one casting office to another, hoping to get past the receptionist's desk and into a producer's office. The anterooms were often grungy and in need of paint, although the walls were hung with photographs of the producer's plays and autographed portraits of players. In the winter, radiators clanked against the cold; in the summer, the rooms were hotboxes. For the very young, all this still had glamour. After "making the rounds," players often gathered in the Astor Drugstore on Times Square to drink sodas and trade tips about who was casting what, and where there might be an opening.

That day I did whatever it was Miss Le Gallienne had asked me to do, and as I was leaving the casting office a young man fell into step beside me. He was shorter than I, but otherwise personable. It was noon and he asked me what I was doing for lunch. My salary wasn't to start till the following week, so I said I was going to the Automat on Fifty-seventh Street, where I could get a sandwich and soup for a quarter. (Subways and buses were a nickel; only the Fifth Avenue double-decker buses were a dime. A hot dog was a nickel; a hamburger was a dime; tea and coffee were a nickel; cocoa, which I preferred, or a glass of milk, was a dime.) The young man told me his name was Paul and invited me to have lunch with him and took me to Fifty-seventh Street, not to the Automat but to the Russian Tea Room, which was a famous haunt of musicians and ballet dancers and was definitely out of my pocketbook range. It represented opera and concerts and ballet and the glamour of composers and singers and dancers. I had played in Chekhov's *The Three Sisters* in college; I was suitably impressed with Paul's choice.

We talked about theatre and theatre people for over an hour, and he, in his turn, was impressed by my forthcoming tour with *Uncle Harry*, though I emphasized that I was a mere understudy. After lunch he suggested a movie, and we went to a rerun of *Grand Illusion*, that magnificent French anti-war movie set in World War I. We remarked on the irony, or, perhaps, the aptness, of this movie's present popularity, and Paul invited me to have dinner with him. He explained that he had a job as a radio announcer in Philadelphia but that he came into New York every month or so to make the rounds and look for a job on Broadway. He would be going back to Philadelphia that night.

I said that I'd love to have dinner with him but that I'd like to change my clothes to something a little dressier than my skirt and sweater. So we took the subway downtown and walked to my apartment, where I suggested he sit in the living room while

I changed. What incredible naïveté on my part, to ask a totally strange man, personable or no, to come up to my apartment while I changed my clothes! Or was it stupidity? "He could have raped you," someone said later. Or was it a sense that this young man was, in the old-fashioned sense of the word, a gentleman and could be trusted? In any event, he sat quietly on my little grey sofa while I changed, and we had the first of many pleasant evenings together. These ended after I introduced him to Hugh.

&. I loved being on the road. Today, when I go off to give lectures, I call it being "on the road." I stay in better hotels than I did when my salary was Equity minimum. Indeed, I sometimes stay at the same hotels that Eva Le Gallienne and Joseph Schildkraut stayed at.

At the first rehearsal for the *Uncle Harry* tour, before we left New York, I felt elated, despite my low status as understudy. I had a real costume, two lines to say, and a steamer trunk which would appear in my dressing room at each theatre in each city where we played. I had my Equity card. I was a professional.

The rehearsal went easily. Most of the original cast were going on the road. We broke up at dusk on a lovely autumn evening, and Mr. Schildkraut came over to me. "Madeleine, darling, would you like to have dinner with me?"

I almost fainted. Managed to stutter, "Oh, y-yes, thank you, Mr. Schildkraut."

I had been told that Joseph Schildkraut was partial to little blondes. If there is one thing I have never been, it is a little blonde. The girl who was being asked out to dinner by this glamorous star was nearly six feet tall, and ever clumsy. My hair was what a young friend calls "hair-colored hair," neither blond nor brown. Not exactly mouse. Just hair. My clothes were clean and tidy but hardly *haute couture*. I was aware that everybody who had heard the dinner invitation was looking at me with amazed curiosity. Mr. Schildkraut handed me into a taxi and we headed toward the Essex House on Central Park South, where he had a suite. In the taxi he chatted about the upcoming tour, the quality of the actors, the cities where we would be playing. I responded in monosyllables.

In the Essex House we went up in an elevator to a high suite overlooking the city. I was amazed that his rooms looked totally unlived in. I had assumed that it was his apartment, that it would be full of his things. But there was nothing personal, not a photograph, not a book, not a flower. Through the open door I could see into a bedroom with twin beds, one bed neatly turned down, with striped pajamas laid across it.

Suddenly I was swept into Joseph Schildkraut's arms, his lips were on mine, and he was kissing me passionately. I froze.

Naïve Madeleine.

I was totally unprepared for this. What had I expected? I don't think I had any idea what to expect. I, the unimportant understudy, was being asked out for dinner with the great star. My expectations went no further than that. I was terrified. Rigid with shock.

Mr. Schildkraut dropped his arms, pulled away, asking, "Darling, you don't want to?"

"Oh, no, please, Mr. Schildkraut," I gasped.

"All right, darling," he replied. "We have dinner and I talk about my father."

Which we did. What might easily have been a terrible trauma

turned into a rich friendship, and Mr. Schildkraut became Pepé. He ordered dinner, which was set out on a small table by the window, from which we could see the bright lights of the city. New York was shortly to have a brownout, its lights dimmed because of the war, but the Great White Way was still bright. While we ate, Pepé told me stories of the great Rudolph. With incredible generosity, Pepé adored his father, telling me plainly that Rudolph was a far greater actor than he. I saw Rudolph only in *The King of Kings*, so I have no way of knowing, only of admiring Pepé for the simplicity of his love. Perhaps Rudolph was a more consistent actor; Pepé, for all his brilliance, was variable, and one never knew what his performance was going to be like. At least it was never static, and if some nights it worked better than others, it was always an interesting performance.

Nearly once a week, during the length of the tour, he would come to me backstage, asking, "Dinner, darling?"

"Of course, Mr. Schildkraut."

"Pepé, darling."

"Pepé," I would reply.

꙳ On a tour, one goes from hotel to hotel. On Equity minimum, I shared hotel rooms with other women, so the tour was a combination of the joy of the professional theatre and being back in a dorm with roommates. But I flourished in the community of the touring company. Thelma, the stage manager, and her assistant took me under their competent wings. They were considerably older than I, and far older in experience than chronology. Somehow or other they managed to protect me from

my own ignorance, while gently instru
tiny as a bird, but the large stagehands w
to do her bidding and held her in great respe

  The tour ended in late spring and my first novel was optioned by the Vanguard Press for three months for one hundred dollars. The manuscript had gone to Vanguard because the publisher, Jim Henle, had been the first of several publishers who had read one or another of my stories in various literary magazines and had written to inquire if I was writing a novel.

I was fortunate at Vanguard to have a fine young editor, Bernard Perry, who later founded the University of Indiana Press. Bernard somehow managed to make me understand what I needed to do with the shapeless mass of material I had given Vanguard, to refine it and tidy it until it became a novel.

I worked hard that summer, and hard work is in itself a protection. I had to get a finished manuscript in to Vanguard by the end of the summer. Idleness was not a problem. I might still be amazingly ignorant in most aspects of life, but I knew how to work. That was probably the most important lesson I learned in college.

Even with hot dogs a nickel and hamburgers a dime, it wasn't easy to live for the entire summer on one hundred dollars. I picked up extra money with odd jobs, and I continued to sell war bonds in theatre lobbies. Since I also saw all the plays, this seemed more a pleasure than a contribution to the war effort, so I became a volunteer at St. Vincent's Hospital on Twelfth Street. The hospital was in desperate need of help. The volunteers trained by doing whatever job had to be done, and in a few weeks

...came the equivalent of the recovery-room nurse, staying with patients after surgery until they were fully out of anesthesia.

This gave me a feeling of real usefulness. Ours was not an ambiguous war (as I had occasion to tell our son and some of his friends during the Vietnam War). Even before Pearl Harbor and the entrance of the United States, willy-nilly, into the war, I had cousins in England who were being bombed by Hitler's Luftwaffe; cousins in France fighting with the maquis, or in Africa with de Gaulle, who was still a great hero for us. I, too, wanted to help stop the megalomaniac in Germany from destroying the Europe I knew and loved, stop him from taking over the world.

Even so, I was limited by my own concerns, my little world of theatre and literature. During that summer I wrote much and ate little.

I left my work on the novel briefly to audition for a role (walk-on and understudy) in the forthcoming production of Chekhov's *The Cherry Orchard*, starring Eva Le Gallienne and Joseph Schildkraut and directed by Margaret Webster. Assured that I would be a small part of this project, I returned to the typewriter.

Before the first rehearsal, I had finished *The Small Rain*, and this first novel was accepted by Vanguard and published. Not only did it have good reviews, it had excellent sales. Vanguard arranged to pay my royalties at the rate of two hundred and fifty dollars a month, on which at that time I could live comfortably (rent was eighty dollars a month), rather than loading all the money on me at once. For the several years the money lasted, I had an assured income.

So I started rehearsals for *The Cherry Orchard* feeling rich indeed, with Equity minimum added to my *Small Rain* money.

According to Peggy Webster's staging, the first act of *The*

Cherry Orchard starts with two young maids carrying a large wicker hamper between them, running across the stage. One of them was to trip and fall.

"Which shall it be?" asked Miss Webster.

"Madeleine, of course," said Miss Le Gallienne.

Three

---

*I*n due time I discovered that I had outgrown my apartment on Twelfth Street. It wasn't that my little walk-up was too small; it was that the kitchen was two gas burners over a small box of a fridge tucked in a closet. Dishes had to be washed in the bathtub, across which a wide board was laid. I loved having friends in for dinner; I longed for a real kitchen. Apartments had become hard to come by in wartime New York. Amazingly, I met a young couple who lived on Tenth Street in the parlor floor-through of a brownstone, and who did not want to cook, would just as soon not have a kitchen. They liked my walk-up. We agreed to switch apartments.

Thelma, the stage manager, and several friends helped me move, so that by the first evening on Tenth Street I was already settled in and at home, pictures hung, books in the shelves, music on the piano. The apartment had a lovely big living room over-looking a small garden used by the basement tenants. There was a marble fireplace, over which I hung my mother's Venetian mirror. The piano, of course, had pride of place, and I played at least a couple of hours a day. There were already bookcases built in on one side of the fireplace, and friends helped me balance the architecture with more shelves on the other side. Helped? I watched, while they built.

To get to the bedroom, which faced onto Tenth Street, one had to go through the kitchen to the bathroom, through the bathroom, and thence to the bedroom. But the kitchen was a real kitchen with a stove with four burners and an oven. There was a real standing refrigerator and a proper sink. One wall was filled with cupboards with two pull-out wooden work shelves. It was a small kitchen but so well conceived that it was beautifully functional. The bathroom had a long, deep tub. No shower, but I have always preferred the relaxation of a hot soak to the stimulation of a shower.

That first night I read until I was sleepy, then turned out the light. Slept soundly. Suddenly I was wakened by a horrible, grinding roar. I sat up in bed, terrified, until I realized that the noise came from a garbage truck. They came by, grinding and gnashing, at five o'clock every morning. After the third or fourth morning I never heard these monsters; they had become a subconscious part of my normal routine.

The Cherry Orchard ran to distinguished reviews but slim houses. The people in the company were friendly enough, but there was none of the intimacy of the group on the *Uncle Harry* tour. I felt that I was only an understudy, a person of little importance. The best thing that came to me was the little dog who had to be bought for the play. Charlotta Ivanovna, the governess, had a dog who was frequently referred to. Of course, all the players in the company wanted *their* dog to get the role. But the noise of the party scene was too much for these pets. At the last moment Touché was bought, a charming grey mop of a poodle when small poodles had not yet been overbred and become nervous and yappy. Touché was a born actress. She loved the noise and confusion of the party scene. She learned her entrances and exits so that Charlotta Ivanovna could time herself by Touché, rather than the other way round. Touché was everybody's pet, but I, as assistant stage manager, was given her care. I was very lonely at this time, having broken with most of my old friends, who had come to represent a way of life which seemed to me irresponsible. Surely Le Gallienne, Webster, and Schildkraut saw my loneliness and decided to give Touché to me.

She was my first dog, the first in a long succession of canine companions. She was friendly with all the company, but in a few days there was no question that Touché was my dog and fiercely protective. She had been bought from a reputable kennel, but she had what was ultimately diagnosed as low-grade distemper. I hand-fed her ground beef, which used up my wartime meat coupons. During the day she wilted in my lap like the dying Marguerite in *La Dame aux Camélias*. In the evening I would put her on her leash, walk her to the subway, then drape her over my shoulders like a fur piece and she, little actress that she was, would lie, unmoving, until we were uptown. We would walk to the theatre, Touché drooping miserably. But as soon as we got to the stage-door alley, up would come her little chrysanthemum of a tail and she would trot into the theatre, her ills forgotten in the delight of being onstage.

When audiences dwindled radically, it was decided to close the show for the rest of the season, and then take it on the road in the late summer. During the intervening months I worked on my second novel and learned about life. I learned that I, at any rate, could not make love where there was no love. I learned to laugh when men suggested to me that I should go to bed with them "for the sake of my art." I learned that much that masquerades as love is undisciplined lust. I learned to be wary of young men who had what Miss Le Gallienne called "the honest blue eyes of the congenital liar."

I learned what it was to be truly lonely. I loved my writing and I loved my apartment, but I had neither the money nor the inclination to meet friends at nightclubs or bars, and spend hours in what seemed a terrible waste of time. Touché and I used to go for long walks together, and I explored a city which was still safe to walk in. It was full of soldiers and sailors on leave. Young men I knew slightly from my visits to Jacksonville came through New York on their way overseas and, rather to my surprise, called me and took me out. From one of these, Norman, a distant cousin, I had my first kiss. (If Pepé had kissed me, I had certainly not kissed Pepé.) So late in life? I was a very slow bloomer.

Norman was in New York for only a few days. He took me to dinner at the Plaza, in the elegant Edwardian Room. Later we listened to the famous Hildegarde sing Noël Coward songs. Then we crossed to the Central Park side of Fifty-ninth Street and got into one of the horse-drawn hansom cabs and clopped through the park. And Norman kissed me. He was going overseas; he might get killed (he didn't); kissing was what was expected of us. We were diligent about it, but it meant little to me and probably no more to him.

With three friends I took acting lessons twice a week from a well-known actor and his violinist wife. His star was in the ascendant when he generously took on some young pupils, and it has gone on rising. He is an old man now, and a great actor. He charged us twenty-five cents a lesson, on the theory that it was not good for us to get something for nothing. I learned a great deal from him.

He and his wife lived in a brownstone in the East Seventies, and on New Year's Eve they gave an enormous party. We young ones were invited to come, hang up coats, serve drinks and food, but also we would be mixing with all the great names in theatre and music. We were thrilled, even though we were too busy being servants to speak to anybody other than asking, "May I hang up your coat?" or "Would you like something to drink?" But we watched, listened, were filled with excitement.

At midnight our host stood on a chair and began giving toasts to the glorious Red Army. That was fine. Russia was our ally. But he didn't give toasts to anybody else. Not to the men and women from the United States who were overseas. Not to the British bravely defending their island. Not to the French trying to save some pride out of defeat. Only to the glorious Red Army. I didn't understand what was wrong, but I knew things were skewed. I felt embarrassed, then unclean. I slipped downstairs, put on my coat, went back to my apartment, and took a bath.

So I was saved, as some of my friends were not, from flirting with communism. At that time it was not only attractive, it seemed to fit in with the teaching of Jesus far more than did Christianity. Share everything with the poor. Keep nothing for yourself that you do not need. Find work for all the unemployed. Why wasn't it as wonderful as it sounded? I don't know how I knew that it wasn't, but I knew. Some of my friends found out in a far more distressing way than at a New Year's Eve party.

I did want to build up a new circle of friends, so I accepted invitations to people's homes. One night I went to a party given by a couple whose living room was filled with tanks of tropical fish. Our host would not allow a glass to remain empty for a moment. If I took a sip of my drink my glass would be refilled if I turned my head. So each time he would refill it, I would slosh some into the fish tanks. When I saw several fish swimming around and bumping drunkenly into each other, I decided that it was time to go home.

Even though I had been disturbed at the New Year's Eve party, I was still politically naïve. I had read about the Spanish

Civil War but it had never touched me personally. Then one evening I went to a party hosted by an artistic couple, a cellist and a sculptor, which affected me as profoundly as the toasts to the glorious Red Army. Suddenly, in an ugly argument between an emotional Spaniard and a cool American, the Spanish Civil War was present.

The young Spaniard's name was Julio. I spoke reasonable French, but no Spanish, and was fascinated by the pronunciation, Hoolio. He was a poet, and his passionate war poem had just been published to critical acclaim, and the party was in his honor. Most of the people at the party were a little older than I, and far more sophisticated, and I stood on the outskirts, a little awed, listening.

Suddenly Julio's voice was raised so that I could hear clearly. "But you cannot say you are an anti-fascist and then say you are a Francoist. That is a—contraception."

People around him began to laugh and Julio looked confused.

"Contradiction," the cool American said to Julio. He was dressed in a pin-striped business suit and stood out in a room full of people in bohemian clothes.

"That's what I said."

Someone asked me a question, and the next thing I heard was the man in the business suit saying, pleasantly, as though talking about his liking for artichokes, "I am a very strong, a very firm Catholic."

A man wearing a Russian peasant outfit murmured to me, "He's a fascist, that Louis. I don't know why he's here."

"Being a Catholic doesn't make him a fascist!" said a woman who had been introduced to me as a French war bride.

"Of course not. His politics, not his religion."

Louis's voice was quiet but carrying. "It is because you are blind, because you are an idealist. It would have been better if you had died in Spain, because you are living in a dream." His tone was still friendly, a trifle condescending.

Julio cried out, waving his hands excitedly, "If I am living in a dream, then you are trying to make it a nightmare."

"Perhaps not all of us are asleep. Perhaps some of us are awake."

I felt uncomfortable, and nearly as confused as Julio.

Our hostess moved into the group and cocked her finger at Louis. "Louis, I shoot you. You're dead. Bang-bang. Go home, you louse. This is Julio's party. You're not to bait him."

Louis laughed and went to the card table which had been set up as a bar.

Julio said, "This is the first time this has happened to me. This man is my enemy. In Spain I would shoot him if he did not shoot me first. But because I am in America, because I am a guest here tonight in your house, I have to sit and talk to him."

"I'm sorry, Julio," our hostess said, kissing the top of his dark head, "but I shot him for you, so it's all right." She seemed relaxed and certain that she was taking care of the situation. I wasn't feeling that sure.

Louis came back from the bar with two glasses of wine, one of which he handed to Julio. The Spaniard looked up at him with blazing eyes. I went into the bedroom and got my coat, said goodbye, and left, feeling that if Louis pushed Julio any further, there was going to be violence.

I walked home through the crisp winter air. Walked home alone. Yes. That was one of the splendid things about working in the theatre in the early forties. When I was invited to a party, *I* was invited. There was no need for anybody to think about an escort. If I said I wanted to bring a young man, that was fine. Mostly I preferred to be on my own. Such solitary walks through the streets of New York, usually well after midnight, are no longer advisable. But one thing has carried over: when Hugh and I give a dinner party we don't worry about balancing men and women. We ask people we think would enjoy each other, and if there are more men than women, or vice versa, it presents no problems. I have met single women in other communities whose lives have been narrowed by their singleness. New York gets a very bad press, but in the world of the arts, at least, the single woman is not left out because there is no man available to her.

So I walked home to Tenth Street alone, the words of the quarrel still burning in my ears. In the morning I almost expected that there would be a news item that Julio had killed Louis. There was certainly murder in his eyes. But if anything happened after I left, I never knew about it.

I took care of my feeling of frustration and incompleteness by writing a short story about the evening. So I learned something about writing and something about living, though there was still a vast amount for me to learn about both.

Four

Summer came, and New York heat. On particularly hot and humid days I would open the door to my apartment, then prop open the door to the building. New York was a reasonably safe city in those days, but I am not sure it was that safe. I continued to work at St. Vincent's Hospital and to sell war bonds in theatre lobbies. Sometimes on my way home after a show I would be accosted by a drunken soldier or sailor, but I would just smile and move out of the way and I never had any real problem. If someone started to be ugly, there was always somebody else around to say, "Is he bothering you?"

And I would take the subway home to my apartment, make some supper, turn to the piano, and play my way back into perspective. I was working on the Bach C-minor Toccata and Fugue (I'm still working on it), Handel's Harmonious Blacksmith Variations (still a marvelous finger exercise), and the Bach Two-Part Inventions. One is never through with the Two-Part Inventions; they are the essential practice needed for the Well-Tempered Clavier.

On unbearably hot nights I would ride the subway downtown to the bottom of the city with a friend, take the Staten Island ferry and cool off in the breeze from the water, then walk home along the docks, too ignorant to know that this is never a safe place at midnight. Again, it may have been our ignorance that protected us.

I saw something of a few young men. Orson grew up in China of missionary parents; he was caught in a confusion of Christianity, Buddhism, and Chinese folk religions. I met him one summer when I was acting in stock on Nantucket Island, and he introduced himself to me through a mutual friend. I went out with him a few times and found him interesting and disturbing. He told me that he had decided to end his life by swimming out to sea at Sconset, the far end of Nantucket Island. He had swum out, far beyond the breakers, and suddenly decided that he wanted to live, and fought the tide and the undertow back to shore, and lay there, spent, for hours.

Suicide was not as common then as it is now, and I had never before known anybody who wanted to die—or who had as great a desire for life. Orson fascinated me, though the chemistry between us was calm. I enjoyed our philosophical conversations, and since he also lived in New York most of the year, we were able to meet reasonably frequently. Our friendship was not romantic, but we talked about music, compared records; enjoyed walking all over the city while we talked about the books we were reading, and what Orson was thinking about God and superstition and mythology and mysticism.

It was a chilling shock one day on Tenth Street when I answered the phone and learned that Orson had gone to the Downtown Athletic Club and jumped out a window. There was no turning back this time. And I asked myself with anguish if he hadn't wanted to change his mind as he plummeted down through the air.

I began to learn that life is a mixture of mutually contradictory feelings. Orson's death saddened me, shocked me, but did not prevent me from being elated when my second novel was accepted, with enthusiasm. But, alas, Bernard Perry was gone. There was nobody at Vanguard at that time to tell me that what I had submitted was an excellent first draft but that my manuscript needed work, a lot of work.

I have been blessed with editors who have pushed and prodded me, made me go back to the typewriter and rewrite and revise. This second novel needed that kind of editorial nudging and didn't get it. Hugh was ultimately to be my fiercest editor, but meeting him was still around the corner.

Despite a widening circle of friends, my solitude often turned to loneliness. I decided ruefully that what I had hoped for in the kind of love that is the foundation for marriage was nothing but an idealistic figment of my imagination.

Through my secretarial work for Miss Le Gallienne I met a Hungarian refugee, a cultivated man who took me to the Metropolitan Opera and Carnegie Hall, introduced me to the music of Bruckner, which I found rather heavy, and to Hungarian fruit soups, which I found rather sweet. One evening he invited me to an elegant and expensive restaurant for dinner, and it was evident that this was to be a special evening. As we ate, he told me that he was married and that he and his wife loved each other. She was a winter-sports instructor and some kind of childhood trauma had made her incapable of normal sexual intercourse. In fact, whenever he attempted to consummate their marriage she had responded by throwing up. They had been to the finest therapists. It had nothing to do with him. It was her specific problem, no matter whom she was with. She fully understood his need for sexual fulfillment, but he had not found a suitable mistress since their flight to America. He assured me that he could put me up in a much nicer apartment than my beloved place on Tenth Street. He could get me an apartment on Park Avenue, give me a mink coat . . .

I told him gently that I enjoyed his company but I did not think I was mistress material. After dinner he took me home, and I never saw him again.

Had I, once more, been incredibly naïve to be totally taken aback by his proposal? I was badly shaken. As was my late-evening habit, I put Touché on her leash and walked over to Fifth Avenue, past Mark Twain's house, past the Marshall Chess Club, where the windows were still lit and I could see the silhouettes of men bent over chessboards. On the corner of Tenth and Fifth is Ascension Episcopal Church. It had been endowed with a fund to keep it open twenty-four hours a day. So I tied Touché in the vestibule and slipped into the back of the church to sit and think. Not so much to pray as to take time to *be*. It was a while, that evening, before I could stop my mind from its chaotic whirling.

Almost every night around midnight (for I kept theatre hours—bed at 2 a.m., up at 10 a.m.), I slipped into the church. I would not have dreamed of going in during a church service. My parents' church had not done well by me. In my Anglican boarding schools I was taught Anglican virtues, all self-protective: do not show emotion; do not grieve; do not ask for help; do it yourself. My father died when I was seventeen and no one told me that it was all right to cry, to hurt. True to my tradition, I carried on, did all the brave things, and repressed my grief.

It was a long time before I learned that Anglican virtues and Anglican theology are barely compatible. But Ascension Church was a special place for me, part of my deepening, along with the piano, the books, and the typewriter, which had once been my father's.

Journal entries for those days were earnest. I was reading as many letters of the great writers as I could get hold of, and copying out the things that touched me closely. Knowing that I would soon be traveling with the *Cherry Orchard* company during the upcoming tour, I read deeply from Chekhov and learned much.

"You must once and for all give up being worried about successes and failures. Don't let that concern you. It's your duty to go on working steadily day by day, quite quietly, to be prepared for mistakes, which are inevitable, for failures . . .

"Something in me protests: reason and justice tell me that in the electricity and heat of love for man there is something greater than chastity and abstinence from meat . . .

"The thought that I must, that I ought to write, never leaves me for an instant."

And I added: Nor me.

The next day I wrote: "Today I sold 'Vicky' to *Mademoiselle* magazine for $200." That was big money.

And I wrote down these words of Thoreau: "Time is but the stream I go a-fishing in. I drink at it; but while I drink I see the sandy bottom and detect how shallow it is. Its thin current slides away, but eternity remains. I would drink deeper; fish in the sky whose bottom is pebbly with stars."

On a hot summer evening I went with an actress friend from *Uncle Harry* to spend the night on her tugboat, anchored off the tip of Manhattan. We went into a dock-front bar, were the only ones there, and were treated to a long soliloquy by the owner, who delighted me by saying of one of his patrons, "He was so stingy he wouldn't pay a nickel to see the Statue of Liberty piss— 'scuse my language."

As I recorded such small events in my journal I was, in effect, writing my own story. What we write down we tend not to forget, and that unique evening is as vivid to me now as it was then.

I quoted again (was it Chekhov?): "If you never commit yourself, you never express yourself, and yourself becomes less and less significant and decisive. Calculating selfishness is the annihilation of self."

And from Plato: "He who having no touch of the Muses' madness in his soul, comes to the door and thinks he will get into the temple with the help of art—he, I say, and his poetry are not admitted . . .

"And there is the madness, too, of love, the greatest of Heaven's blessings."

Slowly I was learning who I was and who I wanted to be with the help of the great ones who had gone before me. Composers, too. After sitting at the piano I wrote: "The thing I love about Bach is the strength and simplicity and shape he gives to beauty. For most of us everything in the world seems to swirl around in an amorphous mass of confusion—even the lovely parts of it. Bach takes its beauty—which is somehow blurred in its looseness—and subdues it to his own great and simple spirit.

"It seems to me that most of us don't know anything about life but its bare facts, and they're all pointless unless they're interpreted. I like the way Bach does it."

After an hour with the C-minor Toccata and Fugue I wrote about "Bach's immense and vital freedom within the tight boundaries of strict form. Perhaps that's why life doesn't drive one mad; it's interesting to see how alive and free one can remain within the limits that are always imposed on one and from which there can be no escape."

Life was not entirely "art." I was very aware of the precariousness of the world. I had lost several friends overseas in the war in Europe. What was even worse was seeing a man I had once known as an insouciant stagehand come home trembling, shaking inwardly and outwardly from the horrors he had witnessed on Okinawa.

I saw more of the unspeakably traumatic results of this war when I was asked to be in a Theatre Wing production of *The Warrior's Husband*. I played one of a dozen long-legged Amazons. Our theatres were Army and Navy hospitals, and then mental hospitals for men who had been shellshocked. These soul-sick patients acted as stagehands for us, and we had been warned that they were apt to walk out if we didn't please them. But they liked *The Warrior's Husband* with its ebullience and humor—and probably the almost entirely female and scantily attired cast.

ᴥ After I had declined to be my Hungarian friend's mistress, I was more than ever convinced that marriage was not going to be part of my pattern. I would write, see friends, write, go to the theatre, write, but ultimately I was going to walk alone.

Nevertheless, I went out with several people. One was a handsome blond man with a great golden mustache, whose wife had abandoned him for a Spaniard, ironically enough named Julio, leaving him with the care of their preschool children. He was nicknamed Cap and he definitely pursued me, and it is a human reaction to enjoy being pursued.

Cap was brought up in various capitals of Europe, a delicate, sensitive little boy. In many ways he never grew up, but he had charm and he kept calling me and taking me out. I was pretty forlorn at that time, and Cap was good for my *amour-propre*. I knew that he liked me; I thought he was handsome; we had a good deal in our backgrounds in common, and he was fun to go out with—but I was completely taken aback when he asked me to marry him.

It was New Year's Eve. I had flu, and I was in bed, wearing a white flannel nightgown, with a piece of red flannel a doctor friend had ordered me to keep tied about my throat. I was lying in the dark, the lights out, in a cold room which a small fire in the fireplace did little to help. Shortly before midnight Cap arrived with a bottle of champagne and some food and then he told me that he was in love with me and wanted me to marry him.

I was fond of him. I wondered whether my ideal of what being in love was like might not be a mirage, and I finally agreed not to say no at once, but to wait six months before giving my answer. I knew long before the six months were over that I couldn't marry him. For one thing, he talked constantly, and it seemed to me that anyone who could love so vocally, who found it so necessary to reiterate out loud the depth of his passion, might not, in reality, be very deep.

But Cap would not take no for an answer. He refused to admit that I had ever mentioned the word "no." Or he would make scenes. Or send the children to climb in my lap, twine their arms about my neck, and tell me they wanted me for a mother—and they were darling children. But the answer was no.

I remember Cap with affection and gratitude. He helped me regain my self-confidence at a period when it was at one of its lowest ebbs, and for this I owe him an eternal debt of gratitude.

When the time came for rehearsals of *The Cherry Orchard*, there was considerable recasting. I think that Eva Le Gallienne and Margaret Webster believed that the brevity of the New York run was due to errors in casting. This time they were going to be much more careful.

The role of Petya Trofimov, the young student who was Chekhov's alter ego, was being recast. The actor who had played the role in New York was admirable, but he did not mix with the company, at least not with the underlings. I had high hopes that a young Austrian actor would get the role, a man I had worked with in small acting groups and admired enormously. We had sat on high stools at drugstore counters and sipped coffee together and talked theatre. Coffee was my idea of a "grownup" drink. I usually drank milk or cocoa and sometimes tea. I looked up to this dark-haired man who was very different from golden-mustached Cap.

When I went to the first rehearsal, in an old theatre on Forty-second Street, my Austrian actor friend was not there. Instead, I saw a very tall, thin young man with black hair and enormous, very blue eyes. I had never seen such eyes. In spite of my disappointment that my Austrian friend would not be playing Petya Trofimov, I realized that this young man was gorgeous, absolutely gorgeous, and assumed that he would be as aloof as the actor who had played the role on Broadway. Petya Trofimov was out of my league.

&. The young man was duly introduced to me as Hugh Franklin, and I was told of some of his other featured roles on Broadway. The rehearsal started, and it was an arduous one because of the major casting changes, but it was immediately evident that this was a much better ensemble than the previous one. Miss Le Gallienne had referred to the actress who played Charlotta as a "constipated actress." This new one was warm and responsive. And there was no question that Hugh Franklin was a fine actor who brought a radiant and youthful idealism as well as talent to the role of Petya Trofimov. Miss LeG and Peggy were obviously happy with this new cast. Thelma was again the stage manager and she, too, not overeasily pleased, was smiling.

The rehearsal had started early, at ten in the morning, and broke at three. To my amazement, Petya Trofimov crossed the rehearsal hall to me and suggested that we get a bite to eat—we had not taken time out for lunch.

The rules of theatre etiquette were very different from the rules of debutante parties in Jacksonville, Florida, but they were rules, nevertheless. Women paid their own way. If a man picked up the tab it meant that something really serious was going on. Hugh and I sat over our hamburgers and milk shakes till nearly two in the morning. Then I paid my share of the tab and he walked me to the subway.

But we had talked for ten hours without noticing the time passing. I let myself into my apartment thinking elatedly, "I have met the man I want to marry."

Gone were any lingering ideas of marrying Cap. Gone were doubts about the existence of real love. I wasn't anywhere near understanding it yet, but I was full of joy.

Five

---

*H*ugh and I saw a great deal of each other. I went up to his apartment on West Fifty-fifth Street to meet some of his friends. It was a studio apartment with a garden—or what could have been a garden—out back. He was only two years older than I, but I felt that he moved in a far more grownup world. His friends were people who had already made their mark in the theatre. I began to realize that I, too, had grown up, with one book successfully published, and another accepted by the publisher.

If it did not cross my dazzled mind to wonder why Hugh Franklin was working in the theatre, rather than being in uniform, it crossed his. One evening after rehearsal we were eating supper together in a small, dark restaurant, and he told me he had wanted to be in the Air Force, but they had turned him down because traces of albumin were found in his urine. He had then applied to the Navy and been rejected there, too. Then he was drafted, and the Army wouldn't have him either. When the American Field Service turned him down he was truly distressed; the American Field Service tended to take anyone who could walk.

Hugh explained that he had been very ill as a child. He did not know whether it had been scarlet fever or rheumatic fever, but it was assumed that this was what had caused the traces of albumin in the urine. Today this would not be taken nearly as seriously, but then the fear was that even a small trace of albumin indicated the possibility of kidney failure. Had medical science known then what it knows now, Hugh would probably have been accepted by the Air Force. A sensitive and intelligent doctor had told him that there was no need for him to panic, that he should just lead a normal life. It was a blow to him, nevertheless. I was already so much in love that I was only grateful for his presence.

We finished rehearsals and the show went on the road and I was happy, although Cap provided unexpected complications. He had refused to accept my answer of no, and he kept refusing it. To my dismay, he followed us to Wilmington. He appeared one morning on the train, having bribed his way into the car in which the *Cherry Orchard* company was traveling. He even went to Hugh's dressing room to talk to him and then went out with us afterwards. I was highly embarrassed, not realizing that it probably did me no harm in Hugh's eyes to be pursued by a man who was both sophisticated and good-looking and boyishly passionate about me.

Suddenly I felt desirable and beautifully feminine. Not only was I seeing a lot of Hugh, not only had Cap pursued me, but there was another tall and handsome young man in a smaller role vying for my attention, Bob Hartung, still a good friend. To my amazement and delight, when we arrived at a train station I had *two* young men carrying my bags. This was heady wine for a young woman who had been the wallflower at coming-out parties, to whom to be feminine meant to be petite, who knew every trick of staying in the washroom as long as possible, even going to such lengths as ripping the hem of my dress so that I could take half an hour or more sewing it up.

It was a good thing that Hugh had some competition from Cap and Bob; Hugh, being Hugh, would not have trusted a girl who came to him too easily. It was also a good thing that my innate shyness and ingrained reticence kept me slightly withdrawn; otherwise, I might not have been able to keep from throwing myself at this dazzling young star.

The *Cherry Orchard* road company had the same wonderful sense of community as had the *Uncle Harry* company, and there were many of the same components: the two stars, Le Gallienne and Schildkraut (and Pepé would still call me and say, "Darling, dinner?"), and Thelma the stage manager. Fiona O'Shiel, who had played the barmaid in *Uncle Harry*, was a luscious young maidservant. Cavada, who had washed the pots and pans on Ninth Street, was also in the company.

Into this circle of friends came Anne Jackson, a very young actress playing Anya. Annie, Cavada, Fiona, and I usually shared hotel rooms, often sharing beds in order to save money. My mother would have been horrified at some of the hotels we stayed in. Redheaded Fiona traveled with a bottle of Lysol, and we frequently had to scrub our hotel bathroom before it was fit to use. Touché, of course, was an added problem. I would write ahead to hotels, explaining earnestly that I had the dog who was in the play, and that she had a major role, while I was a mere walk-on. It seemed that only the most expensive or the most primitively cheap hotels would take dogs. Annie, Cavada, and Fiona were incredibly patient with Touché and me and the fleabags which were often the only places willing to accept us.

Hugh, as a featured player, stayed at better hotels than the lowly understudies and bit players—not the grand emporia of the stars, such as the Drake in Chicago—but at least respectable hotels.

How happy were the early months of the *Cherry Orchard* tour when Hugh and I were, in the old-fashioned phrase, courting! I remember scuffling through the autumn leaves in Madison, Wisconsin, holding hands. I missed seeing a lot of the October glory because of course when I was with Hugh I wouldn't wear my glasses, and I was extremely myopic.

In Madison, the University of Wisconsin treated us to a special rerun of the old Lillian and Dorothy Gish silent movie *Orphans of the Storm*, in which the very young Joseph Schildkraut had a small role. I didn't even have my glasses with me in the theatre and couldn't see a thing. Thelma had a postcard and pricked it with a pin and handed it to me, and I held it to my eyes, one at a time, and so saw a little. It didn't really matter. Hugh sat on one side of me, Bob on the other. We were surrounded by our fellow players. Life was rich. No matter what the future held, this was a marvelous moment.

I remember we spent a Sunday on a riverboat in St. Louis in the unusual warmth of what seemed like a summer evening. And Monday evening after the show Hugh, Bob, and I went to playwright Bill Inge's rooms and talked the night away. Good talk, serious talk, but more about interpreting the events of the human heart in words and music than about the outer events of a troubled world.

When we left St. Louis I remember the soot piling up on the train windowsills like black snow as we sped toward Chicago on a Sunday afternoon, arriving just in time to check in at our hotels and rush out to the ballet. I can still feel the tingle of thrill as the orchestra played a Tchaikovsky overture.

Bach is for me the composer of my heart. The structure of a fugue is far more nourishing to me than the emotionalism of the romantics, but Tchaikovsky played a special part in that autumn and early winter. Not only was there the joy of listening to that lush overture with Hugh, but one of Tchaikovsky's waltzes from *Swan Lake* provided the theme music for *The Cherry Orchard* and was played over and over during the party scene. It became "our" music.

With Miss Le Gallienne and Miss Webster, a play was never "set." Hugh, in his role of Petya Trofimov, kept on experimenting and deepening. He would suggest a new interpretation of a scene, and Miss LeG would say, "Let's try it." After the performance, while I waited for Hugh, I would watch them walking to and fro at the back of the stage, either incorporating what Hugh had done into the play, or else discussing why it didn't work, and planning to try something else, and I took this creative fluidity for granted, not understanding until later how generous and unusual was such openness.

Those of us on the lower rungs of the theatrical ladder were encouraged to work on scenes from other plays in order to develop our acting techniques. We were allowed to rehearse on-stage, although, because of the rigid rules of the stagehands' union, we were not allowed to move any of the furniture. Occasionally we made bold to shove a table or chair out of the way, but we had to be sure we were not caught doing it (otherwise, the stagehands would have had to be paid), and we had to put whatever it was back in exactly the place from which we had taken it.

Two of my more interesting jobs in *The Cherry Orchard* were musical. At the end of the first act I played a small lullaby on a recorder. It was necessary that I be in full costume and visible from at least one seat in the audience; otherwise, I would have had to join the prohibitively expensive musicians' union.

Far more difficult than the recorder was the musical saw. In the second act of the play Lubov Andreyevna, Petya Trofimov, and several others are sitting outdoors in the warmth of a spring evening, and Lubov asks, "What was that? It sounded like a harp string breaking, or a bucket falling in the pit."

Harp strings had been broken, buckets dropped, but nothing had the eerie and nostalgic sound that Miss Le Gallienne sought, until someone suggested the musical saw. This instrument (which looks like an ordinary saw), when curved in just the right way and hit with a padded mallet, gives out a weird, vibrating noise which was just right for the desired effect. It was my job, also in full costume, to sit backstage and tap the saw. The great problem was that if the saw was not hit in precisely the right way, instead of the eerie, wailing musical sound it emitted a dull *thunk*. This happened several times in rehearsal to loud laughter, and I was terrified of making a *thunk* during performance, which would totally destroy the mood of the scene. Somehow or other, this never happened, and each night the eerie wail followed my tapping of the saw.

It was apparent to the company that although I had two young men carrying my bags, something special was going on between the young leading man and the understudy. Pepé noticed it. As well as playing the clumsy maid in the first act, I was a guest in the ballroom scene, and for costume wore a beautiful period ballgown. One evening I was standing in the wings waiting to go on when Pepé came by, lifted the skirts of my ballgown, saw my English schoolgirl's white cotton underpants, and said, "Oh no, darling, those will never do."

The next evening he presented me with a pair of lace panties.

I don't remember whether or not I ever wore them. But I knew that lace panties were not the key to Hugh Franklin's heart. And somehow or other I had the sense not to throw myself at him. I remembered being on a staircase backstage in a New York theatre and seeing a woman, a singer, far more glamorous than I, flinging herself at him. And I saw him pull back.

One night at an after-theatre supper with several other members of the company present, Hugh picked up my bill, and continued to do so. Neither of us said anything about this new development. We were articulate about the theatre, about books, about music, and amazingly inarticulate about our feelings.

Hugh not only picked up my tab in restaurants, he helped me bathe and clip Touché, and walked her with me after the theatre. On the evenings when I was not with Hugh, she would always head for the nearest lamppost—because it was a spotlight, not because it was a lamppost. Touché loved spotlights. On nights when Hugh, of whom she approved, was with me, she took much longer, bless her. We would sometimes walk with her half an hour or more, while inwardly I urged her to hold herself back as long as possible.

The world with civilization as I knew it might be falling apart around us, but I was in love.

෨ In Chicago, where we stayed for several weeks, there were other plays in town, and some of them played on Sunday when we were dark, and we would be given standing room in the back of the theatre. Hugh knew many of the players, and one night after a show we went backstage to congratulate one of his friends on her performance. As we were leaving her dressing room, she called me back in and shut the door and told me that she and Hugh had been very close the year before, but that I should feel free to pursue our friendship; she would not stand in the way. She sounded tolerant and forbearing and a little condescending.

I murmured politely and fled. I had not looked beyond the

moment to Hugh's past. I had not thought about previous women being part of his life, especially one who was far more advanced in the theatre and in life than I was. But Hugh and I were both well into our twenties. I had gone out with other men before I met Hugh; of course he had gone out with other women. Cap had not taken it kindly when I told him that I was in love with somebody else and could not possibly be engaged to him, that my answer was no. So why was I staggered at this encounter?

But the tour continued and I was happy. We left Chicago and went farther west, then turned back toward the Northeast. There are many bright memories of cities, theatres, strange cheap hotels. Because of Touché, it was always a problem finding a hotel, and there's one night of hotel hunting I'll never forget.

It was about eight-thirty in the evening when the train, several hours late as usual, pulled into Baltimore, and we were starved because we hadn't had anything to eat since breakfast. There was no stop long enough for us to dash to a station lunchroom; nobody came through the train with paper cups of coffee and sandwiches. No dining car. We were tired, too, because we'd just done a week of one-night stands, and the prospect of a week, seven whole nights, in one bed was very welcome.

Fiona and I were the only two in the company who weren't settled with friends or relatives or in a hotel, and Fiona wasn't settled only out of kindness to me—and Touché. Even when I wrote ahead and received a confirmation in the mail, I would sometimes arrive at a hotel, with the dog, only to be rejected, confirmation or no. I was very grateful to Fiona.

She had once played a summer of stock in Baltimore and had stayed in a boarding house where she was great friends with the landlady, so for once we weren't worried about finding a room. Touché was as hungry as Fiona and I, so one of the first things we did was stop at a lunch wagon and buy her a hamburger.

Fiona and I had some coffee but resisted the temptation to get a couple of hamburgers for ourselves because we had decided to get settled first, then meet Hugh and Bob for a bang-up dinner, bottle of wine and all.

Baltimore has two train stations, one at each end of the city, but it seemed Fiona's boarding house was very close to the station we had not arrived at. So Fiona led the way. Touché and I followed her blindly. The only thing I was sure of was that I would *never* go back to the dreadful hotel where, on the *Uncle Harry* tour, four of us had shared two very dirty double beds, and where there was a bathtub in the middle of the room with a screen around it—but no toilet. The fact that we paid four dollars a week didn't make up for the discomfort.

"It won't be long now," Fiona said comfortingly after we had tramped for blocks and blocks and Touché was beginning to drag on her leash. "It's a lovely boarding house with great big rooms and it'll be a grand change after all those awful dumps." Fiona is a creature brimful of love, with masses of red hair and alabaster skin, so lovely that most people, learning that we were "in the theatre," asked if we were playing at the Gaiety, or whatever was the name of the nearest burlesque house. She walked along now, her face held up to the soft white flakes that were beginning to fall, humming a little. Touché and I dragged after her, and finally Touché deliberately held up one forepaw and started limping pathetically on three legs, until she got her own way and I picked her up and carried her.

We walked and we walked and we walked and Touché, for all her beauty and grace, grows heavy after a while. Finally Fiona said, "Funny we aren't there yet. This doesn't look like a very nice neighborhood." She hailed a passing man and asked for the address of the boarding house. The man leered at us, his eyes going suggestively from our heads to our feet and back up again in a most unpleasant manner, but he did make it clear to us that we had walked all the way across Baltimore for nothing. Fiona's boarding house was a few blocks from the station at which we had arrived.

Fiona turned red and then white and red again. "I don't know how it could have happened—I could have sworn—oh, please forgive me!" she gasped. If it hadn't been for Touché and me, Fiona would have been safely settled in the Lord Baltimore with Hugh and Bob and most of the rest of the company. How could I help forgiving her?

She flung her arms around me. "Tonight I'll give you the ten-dollar back rub. That's a promise."

Touché, my protector, growled as Fiona touched me. "Angel," she said, "I am not molesting your mistress." And then to me, "What on earth are you going to do with Toosh on your wedding night?"

In a weary hour and a half we were back in what, to Fiona, was familiar ground, and soon we went up the brownstone steps of a very nice-looking house. I didn't care what sort of room they gave us. I didn't even care about dinner with Hugh and Bob. I just wanted to take a hot bath and get into bed.

The boarding-house keeper gave one look at my beautiful, my talented, my adorable Touché, and said they didn't take dogs and couldn't make an exception even for a dog who worked to earn her own living. Fiona cajoled and wheedled with all her Irish charm, and Touché, true to her histrionic nature, stood on her hind legs and danced, but the boarding-house keeper was a hatchet-faced old sourpuss and there was no getting around her. As she was pushing us out the door, she started to coo over Touché. This was the last straw.

"If you refuse to allow my dog into your house, please stop gurgling at her," I said coldly, and stalked away.

Fiona hurried down the steps after me. "Angel, that was rude of you, you know," she said softly.

I was ashamed of my temper, as I always am once it's lost. I reached in my coat pocket and pulled out the typewritten list of Baltimore hotels that Al Finch, our advance manager, had posted on the call board. We started by trying all the hotels in the neighborhood. They were without exception expensive, but that needn't have bothered us, because they wouldn't take Touché anyhow. Finally we decided to forget the size of our pay checks and go to the frightfully expensive hotel where Miss Le Gallienne and Mr. Schildkraut were staying.

"I'm sorry," the manager said, "but we don't take dogs."

"Look here"—I was almost in tears—"Miss Eva Le Gallienne is staying here and she has two dogs. And Mr. Joseph Schildkraut is here, too, and he has three dogs." At this point the hotel orchestra, which we could hear playing dimly in the distance, for some reason began to play "The Star-Spangled Banner." As Touché heard the familiar strains her ears pricked up and, tired though she was, she rose to her hind legs. I relaxed, certain that now we would be shown the bridal suite.

The manager didn't change expression. "I'm very sorry, but we take *no* dogs."

Part of my job as assistant stage manager included walking the dogs of the stars. I looked at him with brimming eyes. "If you keep on telling lies, someday God will strike you down. Come, Fiona. Come, Touché." And we stalked out again.

This time Fiona did not scold me for being rude. Back on the street I turned up my collar and blew my nose. "Here's one that says 'theatrical rates' only a couple of blocks from here."

"Let's go." Fiona started off determinedly.

I ran after her. "Look, Fifi, Toosh and I will understand perfectly if you go on back to the Lord Baltimore. Do go, please, and we'll call you when we find a place and tell you where we are."

Fiona simply continued her brisk pace. We got to the corner where the theatrical hotel was supposed to be, but at the number was an imposing building with a canopy, and we guessed with sinking hearts that the management had changed and the rate would no longer be "theatrical."

"Let's try it anyhow, it's only money," Fiona said.

We went up to the door and were just about to push it open when Fiona clutched my arm in a frantic manner and pointed to a brass plate on the door. In chastely etched letters it announced: CREMATORIUM.

We turned and ran down the steps and I started to laugh. "What," demanded Fiona, "is funny?"

"I was just thinking," I explained, "how they'd have looked if we'd gone in and asked if they took dogs." At least we could still laugh.

We started back to the center of town and the hotels that were nearer the theatre. It was after eleven by now and even the inexhaustible Fiona was on her last legs. We looked for a phone and I finally went into a bar and called Hugh and Bob at the Lord Baltimore to tell them to check our suitcases, which they were keeping for us, and go on to bed. We'd probably sleep in the station or maybe find a church that was open all night. Hugh was properly sympathetic but agreed to leave the bags at the desk, saying that they were very tired and they'd already had something to eat because they hadn't heard from us . . .

They were tired! I thought furiously and hung up.

"What about that hotel you stayed in . . ." Fiona started tentatively.

"Fifi, we simply can't stay there. It's too awful to describe, and Touché would never agree to it."

By midnight we had tried all the hotels on the advance manager's list except one. His comment about this was, "Cheap, but certainly wouldn't recommend it for girls."

It was only a couple of blocks from the theatre, so we decided to try it anyhow. The exterior didn't look too prepossessing. Outside a dirty brown building a large sign in lurid red lights proclaimed: ONE DOLLAR A NIGHT.

Fiona turned to me. "At this point we'll try anything, but this looks like a House, not a hotel."

We went into the lobby. A few exhausted-looking sailors were sprawled in chairs whose springs sagged through torn upholstery. Fiona and I looked at the man behind the desk; his face was the color of parchment; he looked as though he'd been embalmed and then the embalmer decided he wasn't dead after all. On his head he wore a pale pink wig. Out from under it strayed a few damp grey hairs.

"Do you take dogs?" Fiona demanded.

The man giggled foolishly. "Do I take dogs!"

Taking this to mean yes, Fiona continued, "One bed is cheaper than two?" He nodded. "All right. How much for a double bed for one week?"

"Five dollars apiece for the young ladies. The dog can share it with you."

"Let's see it, " Fiona said brusquely.

The pink-wigged man took us up in one of those scary elevators where there aren't any doors and only two walls. "What do you girls do?" he asked.

"We work in the theatre," Fiona said.

"At the Gaiety?" he asked—as usual.

"No!" Fiona was indignant. "We're playing·in Chekhov's *The Cherry Orchard* with Eva Le Gallienne and Joseph Schildkraut."

The pink-haired man looked disappointed, but then his eyes

flickered hopefully. "Either of you by any chance Eva Le Gallienne?" Fiona and I imagined Miss Le Gallienne staying in this particular hotel and burst into laughter.

The little man looked hurt and took us down a dim and dirty corridor and flung open a door with a flourish. "Some sailors been sleeping here today," he said, "but we'll change the sheets for you." He made this sound like a great favor.

"Not just sailors," Fiona whispered, pointing to some bobby pins.

Buff wallpaper with a spider design was peeling off the walls. A lumpy iron bedstead angled out from one corner. The floor was covered with cigarette butts. Fiona and I looked at each other.

"Let me see the bathroom," Fiona said bravely. We were astounded to find the bathroom reasonably clean and reasonably modern. We thought of our bottle of Lysol and nodded.

Fortunately, we weren't too far from the Lord Baltimore. We retrieved our bags and were grateful that most of our things were in the steamer trunks which would be waiting for us at the theatre. We thought of Hugh and Bob, having had dinner, asleep in comfortable twin beds, and felt very sorry for ourselves, and not kindly disposed toward anyone who had not shared our ordeal.

It was after one when we finally got to our room. We were far too tired, hungry though we were, to think about dinner. Besides, what would have been open in Baltimore so late on a Sunday night?

Fiona got out the Lysol and we wearily scrubbed the bathroom and the foot and headboards of the bed and all the doorknobs. Someone had put clean sheets on the bed while we were fetching the suitcases, but the blankets hadn't been changed since the opening of the hotel a couple of centuries before. I spread my coat on the foot of the bed and put Touché's blanket over that.

Fiona and I took baths and then I got Touché's dog biscuits out of my suitcase and the three of us each ate several and fell asleep counting, instead of sheep, the days until we could leave Baltimore for three weeks of one-night stands.

𝕫 Perhaps I remember Baltimore particularly because the hotel was miserable; the early December weather was terrible, sleety and raw. In a department store between the hotel and Ford's Theatre was a life-sized Santa Claus, hands on hips, constantly going, "Ho ho ho."

Hugh's and my blossoming love was a bright contrast to the winter drabness, and the *Cherry Orchard* company was charmed by it. But their overt interest and approval was, as I look back, anything but helpful. Years later one of the company told me that she had overheard Miss Le Gallienne saying earnestly, "Hugh, when are you going to marry Madeleine?" Miss LeG, Pepé, everybody, was shoving me down Hugh's throat.

One day, when the *Cherry Orchard* company boarded a train, Hugh did not sit by me as was his custom, but at the far end of the car. I knew that our friends were looking at us with curiosity and distress. But no one asked, "What happened?"

The next evening Cavada came into our dressing room with a small plaster lamb which looked amazingly like Touché. It was her way of saying, "I'm sorry for whatever it is that's come between you and Hugh."

Oh, but my heart hurt.

It is said that the body does not remember pain. When I fell on the ice in the woods and broke my shoulder, it hurt; it hurt excruciatingly. And yet now that it is mended and functional once again, I don't remember the *feel* of what the pain was like, only that it was intense.

Perhaps a psychic blow produces such pain that it, too, is forgotten once it has healed. I can remember without feeling it the agonizing pain of my broken shoulder. I can remember that Hugh's turning away hurt agonizingly, too, and that even in my pain I knew that I would wait for Hugh to come back to me. I couldn't go running after him, crying out, "But what happened? What's wrong?"

The rest of the tour was not happy for me.

We had Christmas on the road, in Washington, and all I remember of that particular Christmas is that Hugh sent me a present through one of the other girls. It was a pair of pink knitted bed socks. I was furiously insulted.

We got back to New York in the early spring and I returned to my much loved apartment. Touché and I went for long walks. I wrote some stories. Worked on a novel which never came to fruition, probably because it was more about my father than about me, and I was still far too young to understand the complexities of my father. One of my stories was called "The Course of Smoothe Love Seldom Runs True" (I spelled smooth *smoothe* until Hugh taught me the correct spelling). I saw friends. Was determined that no one would know that my heart ached. Was determined that I would not call Hugh or try to get in touch with him in any way.

Six

One day I was sitting at the typewriter when the classical musical station I was listening to was interrupted for a news flash. President Roosevelt was dead.

Like the rest of the nation and the world I was shocked. And as always in time of shock I wanted to talk with someone. I knew that Hugh had admired the President, and without stopping to think I dialed his number. He was home, and fortunately he had already heard the news. I told him how sorry I was, and that I knew how much he had cared about the President. He sounded grateful for the call, though we didn't talk long.

Days and weeks went by and I was adhering to my decision not to call Hugh again. What we had had was over, if indeed it had been anything beyond my own imaginative longings.

But I could not put Hugh out of my heart and I thought a great deal about marriage. I had seen young actresses who, before marriage, were always careful never to go out without full makeup, which often included false eyelashes. Their hair was carefully coiffed, their clothes were whatever was the latest fashion. After marriage they became careless about their appearance, wearing shabby dressing gowns until well into the afternoon, leaving their hair up in curlers, forgetting about their faces. I was never one for full makeup plus eyelashes except onstage, but I decided that in the unlikely event of my marriage I would get up in the morning and dress, fix my hair, put on lipstick. It seemed to me the height of discourtesy to dress as though for a performance until you had your man, and then not bother to try to look your best.

❧ In the early summer Hugh called, inviting me out to dinner.

The next evening I joined him at a restaurant near his apartment on Fifty-fifth Street. He was leaving the following day for a full summer of stock, was subletting his apartment, and would not be back in the city till fall.

But we talked. Not as we had after the first rehearsal of *The Cherry Orchard*, when we were discovering each other, but in a far more intimate way. Hugh told me about his childhood, the friends he had made in college, his aspirations as an actor. He talked far more than I did, and I sat across from him, listening, marveling.

He paid the bill and walked me to the subway. When I got home I thought to myself that a man did not talk that openly and vulnerably to a woman he did not intend to marry.

It was a long summer. I did not hear from Hugh. Miss Le Gallienne, Miss Webster, and Mr. Schildkraut did not have a production planned for autumn. I did not make the rounds. I thought that I needed to concentrate on the typewriter.

Bob Hartung and I saw a good deal of each other, rode the Staten Island ferry, walked home with Touché. Once on our way home we saw a man sprawled out on a doorsill and were both too inexperienced to know that he was dead drunk, not dead, until the passing policeman we summoned enlightened us. We collaborated on a comedy which ultimately was to see an Off-Broadway production. We went to the movies, saw mutual friends. I was not unhappy, but a part of me kept remembering that last conversation with Hugh.

In the early autumn he called me. He was home only for a few days, staying with a friend because he was continuing to sublet his apartment since he was about to go on the road in a Philip Barry play, *The Joyous Season*, with Ethel Barrymore. It was slated for Broadway, but would try out on the road for several months first. He asked me to have dinner with him the next night.

This time we met at a restaurant in the Village, and again we talked. He told me about his friendship with Philip Barry, and his admiration for Arthur Hopkins, the director of the play.

And he told me of his beginnings in the theatre. When he was an undergraduate at Northwestern he became good friends with a graduate student, Walter Kerr, later to become one of the theatre's most distinguished critics. When Walter finished his degree, he went to Catholic University in Washington, D.C., to teach and to direct plays in that university's excellent theatre. Sometimes he would bring Broadway stars down to Washington to play leads. Sometimes the stars were not yet stars. Hugh gained rich experience working under Walter's direction.

One day he got a phone call from a nun in Scranton, Pennsylvania. She explained that she was the head of the theatre department in her college there, and that they were planning to do Shakespeare's *Romeo and Juliet* as their biggest production ever, and they had called Catholic University for advice about getting a Broadway star, and Walter Kerr had suggested Hugh. They would pay all his expenses and one hundred dollars.

To an unemployed young actor, that sounded like a good deal.

A tall young woman named Jean Collins met his train. If he stood up straight, Hugh was six feet three inches tall. Jean was nearly six feet tall and always on the lookout for tall men. Before they reached the college she had asked Hugh to the prom, and thus began a friendship that would endure through the years.

Walter Kerr was invited to the production and came, mostly to see Hugh, but also looking for talent for Catholic University. Walter is not a tall man; Walter looked for girls who were shorter than he. Hugh said, "Walter, I want you to meet Jean Collins. Jean, this is Walter Kerr." And that was that. Jean Collins became Mrs. Walter Kerr, the Jean Kerr who was to write such best-selling books as *Please Don't Eat the Daisies*, and such Broadway hits as *Mary, Mary*.

I, in turn, shared my friends: Cavada, who had washed the pots and pans and was becoming a superb actress; Pat, tall and socially awkward like me, with whom I could talk about anything, and who was to become a distinguished physician.

ᴥ Walter was also responsible for Hugh's friendship with Philip Barry. He had managed to persuade Julie Hayden to come to Washington to play in Barry's *Hotel Universe*. She was already a well-known Broadway star, having made her mark in Sean O'Casey's *Shadow and Substance* and William Saroyan's *The Time of Your Life*. Then Walter called Hugh to come and play the male lead.

Rehearsals were in a big gym, and after rehearsals the actors played with the equipment. One afternoon Hugh jumped up to one of the rings, caught it, and pulled himself upside down. At that moment the rope broke.

He woke up in the hospital with a fractured pelvis, fractured collarbone, multiple bruises. Why he didn't break his neck, heaven knows. Father Hardtke, the head of the theatre department, stood by his hospital bed and said, "The doctor tells me that if we postpone the show a week you'll be able to go on. Julie has agreed to stay. How about it?"

When Hugh got out of the hospital he went to rehearsal in a wheelchair, then on crutches, then with a cane.

And then he was on.

He had big hopes for *Hotel Universe*. Surely with Julie Hayden playing opposite him, he would be seen by Broadway producers. There was no air shuttle in those days; it was several grimy hours by train, but Julie was a big enough draw to bring important people down from New York. This production could mean everything to Hugh's career.

The opening came and went. Nothing happened. As far as he knew, nobody came from New York. He returned to his apartment on Fifty-fifth Street still in pain, feeling sore and depressed.

One day out of the blue a telegram came: CALL ME AT THE THEATRE GUILD REGARDS PHILIP BARRY.

Hugh suspected that one of his friends was playing a joke on him, but he called the Theatre Guild anyhow. Indeed, Philip Barry had been trying to find him. A close friend of Barry's had been at the opening of *Hotel Universe* (she wouldn't have been there at the original opening date the week before), and had called Barry: "I've found your new leading man for you."

And so Hugh got his first big break on Broadway in Philip Barry's *Without Love*. Barry, he said, was all set to have him play opposite Katharine Hepburn, but Kate said that she was far too insecure to play with a totally unknown actor, no matter how handsome and talented. But Barry saw to it that Hugh was given another role, was standby for Elliott Nugent, and was assistant stage manager. Later he played Nugent's role opposite Constance

Bennett. This led to a featured role with Helen Hayes in *Harriet*. By the time Hugh and I met, he was assured of featured roles and he had earned them; he was an honest actor, as well as an excellent one; reliable (on time for rehearsals; did not get drunk); faithful to the intent of the playwright, imaginative in interpretation, not overwhelmed with his own importance.

He starred in Ruth and Arnold Goetz's *One-Man Show*, then went off on the road with Ethel Barrymore. When they played in New Haven, he came back to New York after the show Sunday night and asked me out to dinner on Monday. We came back to my apartment after the meal and talked, and my heart beat rapidly because I knew that this was the night he was going to ask me to marry him.

Just as we were, I felt, approaching the moment, the doorbell rang. Reluctantly I went to answer it, and it was a man with whom I went out occasionally, a physician and psychiatrist who should have had enough sensitivity to know when he was barging in. He didn't. After half an hour or so, Hugh stood up and said he had to leave. The next day he would be in Philadelphia. I didn't know when I would see him again.

My mother came to New York in early November to spend a month with me, to see some plays, hear some music, see old friends. She already knew many of my friends, had met Hugh and hadn't much liked him ("He was too possessive," she said later), but Hugh was on tour with Miss Barrymore and wasn't around.

I was not letting my mother or anybody else know that I was seeing Hugh again. If things weren't going to work out this time, nobody was going to know it. I had worn my heart on my sleeve and everybody had seen it bleed and that wasn't going to happen again.

My birthday was at the end of the month. Hugh wired roses

to me, but Bob also sent flowers and asked me out to dinner; I had calls or presents from a couple of other young men. On the second of December I took Mother to Penn Station and saw her onto the train. It was a Sunday morning. Hardly had I got in the door of my apartment when the phone rang and it was Hugh. He was in New York for the night. Could I have dinner?

I told him that I had just put my mother on the train and yes, I was free. We went to one of our favorite restaurants in the Village, and after dinner he came home with me. We talked. About this, about that. He suggested that we play records, and chose Tchaikovsky's *Swan Lake*.

He picked up a book of poetry off the shelves and began leafing through it, and then read me Conrad Aiken's beautiful words:

> *Music I heard with you was more than music,*
> *And bread I broke with you was more than bread.*

And then he said, "Madeleine, will you marry me?"

🙠 And then we talked and talked. He told me that his mother had promised him his grandmother's wedding band and engagement ring, but that he would buy me anything I wanted. I told him that I would love his grandmother's rings. We talked about our desire for children, for family life. He told me again about his childhood illness, and that because of it he didn't expect to live very long, into his fifties, perhaps. We were still in our twenties. The fifties seemed centuries away. And I would take Hugh for any length of time, no matter how short.

He would be in Philadelphia for another week, but would come again to New York the next Sunday.

It must have been toward morning when he left. I got undressed and into bed, but was far too wound up to sleep. For some reason I reached for a volume of Hans Christian Andersen's fairy tales and read for the rest of the night. We had agreed not to tell anybody about our engagement, except our parents.

I called my mother in Jacksonville, asked her how the trip had been, was glad she was safely home, then said, "Oh, by the way, I'm going to get married."

Poor Mother.

She was, of course, to come to love Hugh dearly but at that moment she was not pleased. She had not been forewarned. She had thought that our friendship was long dust. He was an actor and therefore a bad risk. She knew nothing about his family.

I was furious to learn, later, that she had made some discreet inquiries and been satisfied; now that I am older, with children of my own, I understand better.

As for Hugh's mother, it must have been an equal shock to her when her baby boy wrote to tell her that he was marrying what she called "a bachelor girl," living alone in Greenwich Village, who had written two novels, acted in the theatre, and was an Episcopalian! This last may have been the most bitter blow of all.

What must she have felt when Hugh and I were married in a church with the heathenish name of St. Chrysostom's?

But I loved her son. I might not be able to iron his shirts so that they were fit to wear, in those days before drip-dry materials, but I loved him.

She sent him the rings and Hugh brought them to me, a broad gold wedding band which he would keep until the day of our wedding, and a gold engagement ring with a small diamond in a Victorian setting. He also brought me a pair of gold and topaz (my birthstone) earrings, so that I would have something from him which he himself had bought.

A few weekends later I gave a party, inviting all of Hugh's and my friends, though not mentioning that he was going to be there, or even that he was in town. When everybody arrived, Hugh walked out of the kitchen and we shared our news.

I had hidden my heart well. The astonishment of the group was a delight. But it was not only astonishment at this union of two people our friends had thought separate forever, it was genuine joy that at last Hugh and I had come together, where we belonged.

INTERLUDE

I learned fairly early in my marriage that I did not have to confide everything on my mind to my husband; this would be putting on him burdens which I was supposed to carry myself. When a bride insists on telling her lover *every*thing, I suspect she is looking for a father, not a husband. Some of my life was mine to be known by me alone. But our marriage was ours, belonged to the two of us, and was full of wonderful things, terrible things, joyous things, grievous things, but ours.

Crosswicks is an icon of our marriage, that old house we have loved for forty years. We bought it in the spring of our marriage for the (even then) amazing sum of sixty-three hundred dollars. It was my first real experience with a house.

The place was a mess. It had been a two-family house for fifteen years, though nothing had been done to divide it. Upstairs a sink had been put in one of the four bedrooms, and there was a bathroom. Downstairs was the original kitchen and, in one of the old pantries, a chemical toilet. One family lived upstairs; the other, down. Outdoors, a mess of weeds and bushes had grown up. Power mowers were just coming in, so a lawn larger than a pocket handkerchief was hard to keep up. Few people had washing machines and dryers and freezers and all the kitchen equipment we take for granted today.

The fact that Crosswicks had a bathroom was unusual. Most of the old farmhouses in our neck of the woods had outhouses; many had no indoor plumbing, just a pump in the yard. It was, horrible irony, the Second World War which put an end to the Depression, and slowly the outhouses and pumps were replaced with flush toilets, and hot and cold running water.

Sixty-three hundred dollars was more than Hugh and I could manage. Three thousand dollars was already in a mortgage. My mother, also hungry for a house, loaned us three thousand; three hundred we had. Mother loved the house almost as much as we did, spent every summer there, and named it: Crosswicks. Where the two roads meet. My father's childhood was spent in a small village called Crosswicks; his home was a wonderful old house with a wing that was pre-Revolutionary, and a secret room from which you could look out through the eyes of the portraits hanging in the next room. Everybody in the family loved the place, but nobody wanted or could afford to keep it up, so it was sold early in the Depression.

The name Crosswicks sounded felicitous to us, and Hugh and I were happy to accept my mother's suggestion. I was dazzled by marriage and by the glory of having a house, a real house.

But we learned quickly that the wonders of owning a house are sometimes compounded by unexpected frustrations. My mother used to say that a house is a constant beggar. In an apartment, you call the super or the handyman. At Crosswicks during forty years of marriage, we have done as much of the work ourselves as possible. Wallpapering was not difficult to learn, and we soaked off layers of ugly wallpaper, revealing patches of lovely colonial paper beneath. It was too torn and fragile to save, so we put on new wallpaper copied from the patterns of two centuries earlier. Because of the settling of the house, each strip of paper had to be aligned with a homemade plumb line. But the results were spectacular. Our original bedroom still has the very first paper we ever hung. The guest room, which used to be the baby's room, still has the considerably more expensive paper we hung when I was pregnant with our son, Bion.

We attempted nothing electrical. The first major project was having the house rewired, because we were afraid of faulty wiring in a house built and clapboarded with wood. Neither of us is much in the way of plumbing, though we did do things for which in New York we'd have called the super.

One summer early in our living at Crosswicks, a stage-designer friend came with his wife for the weekend. One morning he broke an ashtray and tried to flush it down the toilet. The result was total blockage. Hugh and I watched in awe as neighboring friends showed us how to drain the toilet, unscrew it from the floor, lift it, retrieve the china pieces of the broken ashtray, and put the toilet back together again.

For a while we had a sign warning, PLEASE DO NOT PUT ASHTRAYS DOWN THE TOILET, but it was not a frequently made mistake.

Hugh learned the hard way that sanding ancient, rippling floors covered with layers of paint is best done by a professional. I spent a week with my mother in Florida, and Hugh came up to the country and rented a sander, planning to sand all the floors. By the end of the week he had barely managed to do one room, and his hands were a mess of blisters.

Crosswicks is not a perfect house. It has suffered from wear and tear and years of neglect. The walls and floors are crooked. There is no way to weatherproof it so that in the winter moles and field mice do not seek and find entrance. So throughout the years we have had cats, varying in number, because it is in the nature of cats to keep rodents out of their house.

Some of the rooms need a second wallpapering, some a third. About a quarter of a century ago we reupholstered the living-room furniture—I still think of it as new. Babies and animals have stained the rugs. But Crosswicks is comfortable, warm, welcoming. Friends coming in for the first time have frequently remarked, "What a loving house!"

And so, I hope, are Hugh and I, in our own human and fallible way. We were not a latter-day Héloïse and Abelard, Pelléas and Mélisande when we married. For one thing, the Héloïses and Abelards, the Pelléases and Mélisandes, do not get married and stay married for forty years. A love which depends solely on romance, on the combustion of two attracting chemistries, tends to fizzle out. The famous lovers usually end up dead. A long-term marriage has to move beyond chemistry to compatibility, to friendship, to companionship. It is certainly not that passion disappears, but that it is conjoined with other ways of love.

We have both, throughout the forty years of our marriage, continued to respond with excitement to the same beauty—for instance, to certain pieces of music. I remember driving up to Crosswicks one early spring day when we heard, over the car radio, the beautiful flute solo from Gluck's *Orfeo*, and our response of delight was such that it has always been special music for us. On a cold and dank day we walked along a beach in southern Portugal, arm in arm, gazing with awe at the great eyes painted on the prows of the fishermen's boats. One night we stood by the railing of a freighter and were dazzled by the glory of the Southern Cross against the blackness of an unpolluted sky. If this kind of simultaneous recognition of wonder diminishes, it is a sign of trouble. Thank God it has been a constant for us.

Love of music, of sunsets and sea; a liking for the same kind of people; political opinions that are not radically divergent; a similar stance as we look at the stars and think of the marvelous strangeness of this universe—these are what build a marriage. And it is never to be taken for granted.

Periodically during my life I have needed times of assessment, of stepping back from my life, our life, and contemplating. When I was twenty-nine I wrote in my journal that I did not expect to die soon, but if I did, at least I would know that I had lived.

That was at twenty-nine, when I had been married for two years. It is far more true today when thirty-eight more years of marriage have been added. This is a summer for reviewing and reassessing. My husband is ill and I do not know how it is all going to end.

Of course we never do.

II

---

*TWO-PART
INVENTION*

One

While *The Joyous Season* was still in Washington, D.C., the understudy discovered that she was pregnant and asked to leave the show. Eagerly I applied for the job, and read for Arthur Hopkins. Hugh said earnestly, "Don't give her the job just because of me."

I replied, slightly huffily, "I think I can get it on my own merit," and was accepted, after my reading, by this great director.

I joined the company right after the first of the year, and I don't remember in what city we were playing, just my introduction to Miss Barrymore. She smiled at me warmly and shook hands. "What have I seen you in, dear?"

"Oh, nothing, Miss Barrymore. I'm always an understudy and nobody ever misses a performance."

"But I know your name, dear!"

Hugh said, "She had a book published last year, *The Small Rain*."

Miss Barrymore bathed me with the graciousness of her smile. "That's it! I liked it so much that I bought it for my personal library."

So, before Hugh and I were married, I had had my first novel published, and the second was in galleys. When Hugh asked me to marry him, he knew that I was a writer, that I was not going to give up writing in order to become the perfect housewife. That was important—that Hugh knew who I was. He was as pleased as I at Miss Barrymore's approval of *The Small Rain*.

In mid-January we reached Chicago. This time I was getting ten dollars more than Equity minimum, and stayed at the same hotel as Hugh. I roomed with Liz, one of the women in the company, sharing a bed, as usual, to save money. Hugh shared a bed with one of the men in the show and we (of course) wanted to share a bed together. In those days one didn't just shack up, one got married.

So on the first Sunday in Chicago, when our theatre was dark, we wandered around the Near North looking for an Episcopal church. It was a cold and beautiful day, and we walked until we came to a church with the name of St. Chrysostom's. We went into the beautifully ordered grounds, and met two well-dressed men coming toward us down the path. When they saw us they stopped, and one of them said to Hugh, "I beg your pardon, but aren't you Martin?"

Yes, Martin was the role he was playing in *The Joyous Season*. We went with them to a lovely apartment on Lake Shore Drive, and the rector was called, and an appointment made for us to see him the next day.

He greeted us and had us sit down, and we told him that we'd like to be married. He asked us our names, our ages. I was twenty-seven, Hugh twenty-nine. He asked us if we'd ever been married before. Or divorced. When we said no, he went ahead with the plans for the next Saturday. The brief encounter with the rector was the extent of our marriage counseling. Would we have heard if we'd been given what is now the customary instruction? I'm not sure.

What I am sure of is that we took our marriage vows seriously.

 § Hugh and I were married at St. Chrysostom's Church on January 26, 1946. It was eleven o'clock on a Saturday morning. Standing up with us was a college friend of Hugh's who had sent us a telegram, MARCIE TOO BIG FOR SMALL WEDDING. Marcie was due to deliver their second baby, but Bill was there, and Liz, with whom I had been rooming.

There in the chapel of the church, Hugh and I made promises, promises which for forty years we have, by some grace, been able to keep. We promised to take each other as "wedded husband and wife, to have and to hold from this day forward, for better for worse, for richer for poorer, in sickness and in health, to love and to cherish, till death us do part."

Rings were placed on our fingers, Hugh's grandmother's broad gold ring on mine. Platinum wedding rings were in fashion in the forties, so we had to go to a shop which I remember as a pawnshop to find a matching gold ring for Hugh. These rings were the symbol of the mighty promises we had just made.

After the marriage service there was a luncheon at the Edgewater Beach Hotel, where we were to have the bridal suite for one night. Neither Hugh nor I could eat much. Afterwards we went back to the theatre for a matinee and an evening performance. We must have eaten dinner somewhere, somehow, between the two shows, but my memory doesn't pick up again until the bridal suite, which had a sitting room with soft couches and elegant lamps and a deep-pile carpet. Hugh had ordered champagne and sandwiches. I went into the bathroom, which was full of white tile and which had a large tub and many fluffy white towels, and bathed slowly, luxuriously.

It was a good wedding night.

Two

---

*N*ow at night I am alone. Hugh is in the hospital. I kiss him good night, and go on home to Crosswicks without him. It is very different going to bed alone now rather than because one of us is away for a show or a speaking engagement. In the middle of the night, those strange early hours, one, two, three in the morning, what the Scots call "the wee smas," I tend to worry.

I project into the unknown future, give in to fear, and that is never a good thing to do. I try to turn my mind away from panic and toward hope for the future. We have recently started a new career, a wonderful one which came about because I was asked to give a talk at the Library of Congress; while in Washington I made a tape for the Voice of America. Shortly after I got home I received a letter from the U.S. Information Agency asking if I would like to do some traveling for them, as a cultural representative. Of course!

But then, a few weeks before I was scheduled to go to Egypt, I fell on the ice while I was walking in the woods, and broke my shoulder.

A broken shoulder not only incapacitates your arm (my right arm, in this case, and I am right-handed), but all of you. I could not do my usual leap up onto our high four-poster bed (where now I toss and turn) but had to use a stool. Try getting up off a low seat with a broken shoulder. Try pulling on panty hose. Try fastening a bra. And there was Egypt coming up!

There was no way I could possibly travel alone, and Hugh was free to go with me. The Embassy in Cairo had asked for a writer, but they really didn't know what they wanted me to do, and were delighted with the idea of an actor and a writer working together. After our first "performance" there was no question that we were to be billed as a team. It is much easier for an audience whose English may well be rudimentary to respond to two people whose body movements and facial expressions add meaning to the words, much easier than to listen to one voice, and our readings were wondrously successful. We were good together, not only as actors, but in what we put across as human beings. It is good for the audience to see husband and wife communicating, working together in easy camaraderie. What we were hoping to do with the readings was to make connections, in the belief that what connects us human beings is far more central than that which separates us, and the response was marvelously affirming.

I turn now in the big bed, from one side to another, my mind still tense. Where will we go next? Will we go?

We are just back from China, a wonderful trip for most of April, returning home in early May.

Egypt. Portugal. China. What jet-setters we sound like. But we had been married for twenty-five years before we had more than two nights away together. When Hugh started to play Dr. Charles Tyler on television in *All My Children*, we began to get real vacations. When a play closes you don't go on vacation, you're out of work. So our holidays have been a special pleasure, since we've waited so long for them.

We've been back from China less than a month. Our last stop on this trip was Hong Kong, where we gave a reading at the Embassy Library.

The whole trip was a special joy, but even before we left for Beijing I was worried about Hugh. He seemed thin and frail and I was filled with anxiety that something might happen to him while we were far from home. I did not voice my fears or write about them in my journal, because that would have given them a reality I desperately desired to avoid.

But we had a beautiful trip, happy and comfortable together, happy and comfortable with our group, though there was for me a steady undercurrent of concern. Hugh, however, was at his most relaxed, at his most charming and witty. And the undercurrent of concern was conjoined by a flowing river of love, love for each other after forty years, a richness of love which we both felt.

Occasionally we would drop out of the activities for a few hours, just to enjoy quiet time together, walking in the cool spring air, holding hands. Mostly it was an active trip, mixed with study and sightseeing. It happened that we were in Xian at the time of the bombing of Libya, and we were very aware of the strong anti-American reaction. I stood in the lobby of the Golden Flower Hotel in Xian with a copy of *China Today* and read with a sinking heart what it told about the United States, my country, dropping bombs, and shook my head in dismay. Our beautiful National Guide looked at me, asking, "You do not like this war?"

"No. I think it's terrible. You do not cure terrorism by terrorism." And then I added, "Not all Americans feel the same way, you know."

Thank God. In the United States we are still allowed to have radically varying opinions and still remain fellow Americans.

A few days later this young Chinese woman and I happened

to be alone for a few minutes outside an ancient temple. We sat on a stone wall and she stated, "You have a very happy marriage."

"Yes."

(Our river of love must have been visible to her.)

"How long?"

"Forty years."

And she made little murmurings of awe and approval.

&. The bombing of Tripoli, breaking into the peace of our China trip, was a potent reminder that this has been a century of war, one war after another, and that seems to have been the way of this planet, as my childhood fears of war keep coming true.

During the Peloponnesian Wars, which lasted from 431 to 404 B.C., Aristophanes wrote: "O thou that makest wars to cease in all the world in accordance wtih thine ancient Name: we beseech thee to make war and tumult now to cease. From the murmur and subtlety of suspicion with which we vex one another give us rest. Make a new beginning, and mingle again the kindred of nations in the alchemy of love, and with some finer essence of forbearance and forgiveness, temper our minds."

That prayer is as apt now as it was then. Why can we not heed it?

The Chinese understand hot blood better than cold blood, and so do I. We were told by our guide about a domestic Chinese plane that had been hijacked. The passengers overwhelmed the hijackers and beat them up. They were taken off at the next stop and executed. There have been no more internal hijackings in China.

Hugh and I saw this hot-bloodedness in a department store

in Shanghai where a man tried to snatch a woman's purse. The other shoppers jumped on the man and took the purse and hit him. Immediate retribution.

In the French legal system a distinction is made between a murder committed in hot blood and one in cold blood.

Coldness of heart has never been (or should never have been) a Christian attribute. It was coldness and hardness of heart that angered Jesus.

Not that I am advocating violence, or excusing it. But I remember George MacDonald's writing that it may be infinitely worse to refuse to forgive than to murder, because the latter may be the impulse of a moment of heat, whereas lack of forgiveness is a cold and deliberate choice of the heart. Not that I'm excusing murder, either! But all this made me do some thinking about marriage (rather than war), making me remember some households where I was intensely uncomfortable because the husband and wife chipped at each other. When Hugh and I get angry at each other we tend to be explosive, both of us being volatile. But we never nibble or chip. And our anger never lasts beyond bedtime. When it happens, and I suspect there's no marriage where it doesn't, it's a good, clean anger, clearing the air. The explosions are not physical, but they are volatilely vocal. And I am reminded of one woman who, when asked if she had ever contemplated divorcing her husband, replied, Divorce, never! Murder, yes!

As the years have moved on, our explosions have become far less frequent as we have learned to live with each other, accepting each other's edges and corners. Sometimes idiosyncrasies which used to be irritating become endearing, part of the complexity of a partner who has become woven deep into our own selves.

While Hugh and I were in China we wanted to be good cultural representatives of our country. Perhaps the best thing we did was simply to stand still, surrounded by a group of curious people, and let them touch us. Before leaving for China we had read that Chinese culture prohibits demonstrations of affection in public, so we were not prepared for people to pat and pet as they did—and especially Hugh, whose huge blue eyes fascinated the dark-eyed Chinese. They would reach out eager hands, and someone would manage to ask Hugh how old he was, and he would sign, "Sixty-nine," and then there would be little strokings and murmurings of approval.

I wanted to buy him a Mao jacket, because I thought he would look gorgeous in one. Our National Guide took us one afternoon to a big Chinese department store, not one of the Friendship Stores designed for tourists, but a real Chinese store, where we would have been completely lost without our guide. She led us to the right department and suddenly Hugh was surrounded by a crowd of Chinese people, all of whom encouraged him to try on various Mao jackets and nodded their approval as he put on the most expensive one in a soft blue wool which brought out the color of his eyes. There was no question that this was the one they wanted him to buy.

He wore it that night for dinner. We were not sure that this would be approved by the Chinese; maybe they would resent a "round-eyed devil" wearing such a jacket. But he was met with smiles of approbation and appreciation.

⋙ Will he ever wear it again?

It is nearly dawn and I am still awake.

The house moves in its sleep, as old houses tend to do. Bion and his wife, Laurie, are, I hope, asleep. Now that they are living full-time at Crosswicks, Hugh and I can be here more often than when we had to close the house for the winter. A house needs to be lived in, and Bion has taken over the heavy work, storm windows, wood chopping. He teaches English at the nearby branch of the University of Connecticut. Laurie is a physician, an internist, with an office in the village, and is on the staff of an excellent hospital in nearby Torrington, Charlotte Hungerford Hospital, where Hugh is this night.

It is a good hospital. The prognosis for Hugh is good. Why can't I sleep?

Immediately after our return from China, I had set off on a spring lecture jaunt. Hugh stayed at Crosswicks. Ever since we have been able to afford to, we have called daily when we are apart. When I called Hugh from New Orleans I sensed something wrong, and his reassurances did not reassure me.

The night I got back to Crosswicks and we were getting ready for bed, Hugh told me that he'd spoken to Laurie, and that he had an appointment with a urologist. He'd had frequent urination, and Laurie said it seemed like a prostate problem.

The afternoon of his first visit to the urologist, he was whistling as he came through the garage. There was nothing to indicate malignancy. Hugh was to have an X-ray early the next morning, and then another appointment with the urologist, who would do a cystoscopy. The expectation was that the doctor would scrape the prostate from the inside to widen the opening. Hugh would likely be in the hospital for five days, then be home for two weeks doing nothing—which would knock askew a number of plans, including our week doing readings together at Laity Lodge in Texas. But all I cared about was having Hugh be well.

We sat and talked that evening, according to our usual pattern, as we prepared for sleep. We were happy, making plans, wondering where our next trip would be. There had been a suggestion by the USIA that we go to Poland and Yugoslavia, and we agreed that this would be fun, even if they decided to send us during the winter.

It is nearly dawn. The birds are beginning to sing.

Will there be another trip?

Three

*H*ow we have enjoyed our travels together! But right now thoughts of a new trip are set aside.

Hugh saw the urologist for the cystoscopy on the thirtieth of May. He found a growth in the bladder and will not have the results of the biopsy till Monday. So fear, which was lifted for a few days, has fallen on us again.

Herb, the urologist, told Laurie that the growth in the bladder was completely unexpected. It's very small, and unrelated to the enlarged prostate. So Hugh's mild prostate problem may prove to be a blessing in disguise, since it caused the growth to be discovered while it's still too small to have caused symptoms. The best we can hope for is that it's not malignant. The next best is that it is small enough just to be scraped out. Hugh is extremely good about it, but it is a terrible blow.

I call several close friends to ask for prayers.

That afternoon Hugh and I have to attend the funeral of an actor friend, here in our Congregational Church. As we approach the white-spired church we hear the mournful sound of bagpipes, and in front of the church is a man in kilts, playing a dirge. My skin prickles.

We go in and I sit beside Hugh, and we hold hands, as the bagpipes continue to drone mournfully outside. I have to clench my teeth to keep from crying.

And I am praying, praying.

When I went to New Orleans (so short a time ago), I took a small paperback book a friend gave me over a year ago. *When Bad Things Happen to Good People*. It is a fine book by one who has gone through the fire. The writer watched his young son die of a dreadful disease in which a child grows into an old man and dies of old age—at fourteen, in the case of Rabbi Kushner's son. He asks all the hard questions and addresses them honestly. In two places I feel very differently from the way he does. He is a man, and a rabbi. I am a woman, struggling with an incarnational view of the universe.

I write in my journal: "He writes that if a God of love allows terrible things to happen to innocent people, then God must be powerless. I can't believe that the power that started the glories of the galaxies ever loses power. But we human beings have free will, and disease is a result of our abuse of that free will throughout the centuries.

"He also writes that there are prayers that one is not allowed to pray, such as my 'Please, dear God, don't let it be cancer.' Rabbi Kushner says I can't pray that way, because right now either it is cancer or it is not.

"But I can't live with that. I think we *can* pray. I think the heart overrides the intellect and insists on praying."

If we don't pray according to the needs of the heart, we repress our deepest longings. Our prayers may not be rational, and we may be quite aware of that, but if we repress our needs, then those unsaid prayers will fester.

The funeral of our friend is painful. In a small, closely knit village, someone always asks, "I wonder who will be the next to go?"

We come home from the church. Herb has called to say that there is a malignant tumor in the bladder but it is inconclusive whether it is little and easily removed or whether it has spread. Oh, God. Since Hugh has had no blood in his urine we can legitimately hope that the cancer is little and will be easily removed. He is to go into the hospital tomorrow to have surgery on Wednesday.

I am scheduled to lead a conference at nearby Trinity Conference Center in Cornwall just the days that Hugh is to be in the hospital. It is much too late for a replacement to be found for me, so I make some rather frantic phone calls, explaining that I'll have to commute between the Conference Center in Cornwall and the hospital in Torrington while Hugh is there. I feel terribly torn, but I know that I can't be at Hugh's bedside all the time, and if I'm working when I'm not at the hospital, that will keep me from worrying. No matter how simple we hope the surgery will be—oh, let it be simple—it is still cancer, and I am very frightened.

I think again of my concern before and during the China trip. But the China trip was a joy and I thought I was wrong.

And then this comes out of the blue.

How well I understand the childish prayer: "Oh, God, make it not to have happened. Take it back."

And so I pray as my heart needs to pray. Divide my time between the Conference Center and the hospital. The conference is for a group of a dozen or so clergy wives. I was with them a year ago, warm, wonderful women with a wide range of interests and age. I am close enough to them so that I can talk about prayer in times of stress.

Hugh's surgery is on the fourth of June. I spend the morning giving a talk at the Conference Center, since I cannot be with him during surgery or in the recovery room. I spend the afternoon with him. He is only slightly groggy, is very much with me, but snoozes a good deal of the time.

Bion comes for me, to drive me the half hour back to the Conference Center. He tells me in the car that the surgery wasn't as simple as we had hoped. The cancer has spread, and Herb thinks he'll have to remove the bladder. Chemotherapy, too. I am stunned. Laurie says that it is not a death sentence. There is real hope. But I feel a deep interior chill, and try to keep my body from trembling.

I ask Bion to let me off at the road which leads to the Conference Center, and I walk the mile or so there, pulling myself together. The afternoon sun is hot, but all I feel is cold.

The Trinity wives are waiting for me, expecting me to bring good news. When it is bad, their arms open.

At bedtime, in a cold, strange room, I read Evening Prayer. Read the first Psalm for the evening of the fourth day: "My God, my God, why have you forsaken me?"

Exquisitely painful timing. The psalmist's words. Jesus' words. I feel anguished. I feel that I have been kicked in the stomach and the wind knocked out of me. My spirit hurts.

I am grateful that Jesus cried out those words, because it means that I need never fear to cry them out myself. I need never fear, nor feel any sense of guilt, during the inevitable moments of forsakenness. They come to us all. They are part of the soul's growth.

In this room at Trinity Conference Center I am part of a community. At home I am surrounded by the community of family. Bion and Laurie are deeply involved in this crisis. Tomorrow my daughter Josephine, her husband, Alan, with their nine-year-old son, Edward, are arriving for the graduations of their daughters, Léna and Charlotte, from high school, one day apart. Charlotte, fourteen months younger than Léna, accelerated herself and is graduating a year early, a day before her older sister.

When Alan accepted the job of dean of Grace Cathedral in San Francisco a year ago, the bonus for Hugh and me was that their two girls were finishing school in the East. For much of the school year Léna lived with us, and Charlotte came for frequent weekends.

When Léna moved in, Hugh said, "There will be rules."

Léna blanched.

I said firmly, "The rules are these. You do not drink up your grandfather's grapefruit juice so that he has none in the morning. Rule two is that when you are going to be late, you telephone. Those are the rules."

She thought she could live with those.

Later I added a third one: "When you empty an ice tray, you refill it."

The two girls will be living together in our apartment this summer, with jobs to help toward college in the autumn. Léna will be going to Barnard, Charlotte to a new four-year liberal-arts college at the New School for Social Research. It is good to have them with us.

I am close to our younger daughter, Maria, on the phone. She is pregnant, nearly ready to deliver her second baby. I am surrounded by the community of family. Out of this pain there is a strangely sustaining unity.

❧ By some small marvel it happens that a family very dear to me is visiting in the East. Ed is an oncologist, and has just been at a medical conference with particular emphasis on bladder cancer. He and his wife, Jan, and their little ones come by to see us and to talk with great love and concern about the proposed treatment for Hugh. Ed brings material on the latest, very new treatment for bladder cancer, platinum chemotherapy, which seems to hold out real hope for cure. Ed is relieved to learn that this is exactly what the doctors—Herb, the urologist, and Michael, the oncologist—have planned for Hugh. The treatment is still so new Ed had been concerned that it might not yet be used at Charlotte Hungerford Hospital, and he had wondered how to tell us that this is what should be done. He says that he has studied Hugh's case prayerfully, and if it were his father, this is the treatment he would prescribe.

The doctors are confident. The cancer has been discovered pre-symptomatically. They, too, tell us of the amazing success of the new treatment. But I am grateful for Ed's reinforcement of the decision to use platinum, because the treatment is terribly toxic to the rest of the body.

Hugh is moved from his room on the fifth floor of the hospital, down to the third floor, the cancer floor. He is put in a semi-private room, but there is nobody else in it, so I am able to be with him all day. There is no private bathroom and he has to walk down the hall pushing his IV pole with one hand, carrying his urine bag in the other. He is weak and terribly nauseated.

There are other patients on the floor far more ill than he. The floor is like an odd T, with a large crossbar, which has the cancer rooms, and a smaller long bar, which is the psychiatric wing, a depressing combination. But the cancer nurses are kind and patient and particularly skilled in giving the chemotherapy IVs.

Carol, who helps keep Crosswicks clean, begs me, "Keep your

faith." And I reply, "Oh, yes, I will. I am." And I am. But what do I mean?

This summer is teaching me what I mean.

৯ When the urologist told us that Hugh's cancer was far worse than he had anticipated, he said, "I feel as though I've dropped an atom bomb on you."

I feel that way, too. Blasted. And stuck with that problem of free will I care so much about.

As a human parent I have had to allow my children to make their own mistakes, to become free adults. I cannot rush in and correct every error in judgment, fix everything that goes wrong. Parents who attempt to do that usually end up with children who grow into emotional cripples. If we accept that we have at least an iota of free will, we cannot throw it back the moment things go wrong. Like a human parent, God will help us when we ask for help, but in a way that will make us more mature, more real, not in a way that will diminish us. And God does not wave a magic wand and clean up the planet we have abused. Our polluted planet is causing more people to die of cancer than when the skies and seas and earth were clean.

My head understands this. My heart still cries out. And I remember my seventeen-year-old prayer on the train from Charleston to Jacksonville when my father was dying: "Please, God, do whatever is best for Father. Please do whatever is best for Father." And that, of course, underlies all our praying. Do what is best, even if at this moment I cannot know what that best may be.

I sit in the hospital room with Hugh. This is his third room and each room has an original painting on the wall. They vary radically in quality. The first was a still life with apples; the second a beach with ocean waves; here on the cancer floor it is a picture of three golden retriever puppies, not unlike our own two goldens. I sit by the bed, hold Hugh's hand, try to help him eat when meals are brought in. That is all I can do. Try to affirm with quiet love, a love that has built slowly over forty years.

Our love has been anything but perfect and anything but static. Inevitably there have been times when one of us has outrun the other and has had to wait patiently for the other to catch up. There have been times when we have misunderstood each other, demanded too much of each other, been insensitive to the other's needs. I do not believe there is any marriage where this does not happen. The growth of love is not a straight line, but a series of hills and valleys. I suspect that in every good marriage there are times when love seems to be over. Sometimes these desert lines are simply the only way to the next oasis, which is far more lush and beautiful after the desert crossing than it could possibly have been without it.

* Not long after our marriage I wrote in my journal: "I read somewhere that one appreciates happiness only when one is afraid of losing it. But in the world today one has to accept that fear as a kind of guest in the house and it makes the moments when it is pushed into the background more intense and more wonderful. And what one has had, as long as there is life and reason in one's body, can never be taken away."

After our glamorous night at the Edgewater Beach Hotel bridal suite, we went back to the old Croyden Hotel, where we had a long room with a sofa and a couple of old but comfortable chairs, and a Murphy bed that folded up into the wall in the morning. We had a sizable dressing-room-cum-kitchen, and a bath. In the evenings after the theatre I would bathe and lie in bed, waiting for Hugh, and looking with dazzlement at my rings.

We rented a radio and found one hour a day of classical music. We had friends from our company, and from others playing in Chicago, in for dinner, which I cooked on two burners—it was not unlike the closet kitchen on Twelfth Street, but it was more fun.

I wrote stories, and in my journal I wrote a lot, anguishedly, about the world situation. Sometimes it is not a bad idea to remember that it was as bad then as it is now.

After the play closed in Chicago, Hugh and I bought a very secondhand car. It had a gearshift which kept flipping back into neutral, so that we had to drive through the Ozarks with one hand holding the shift in gear. We were en route to visit Hugh's family in Tulsa, stopping to see friends and family along the way. While we were in Jacksonville with my mother she gave a large reception for us, and I couldn't help being pleased as this ex-wallflower's husband was admired. Tall, handsome, and unfailingly courteous to the old ladies, who adored him, Hugh made a big hit.

After a week with Mother we headed North. We stopped off in Washington with Walter and Jean Kerr. Forty years later Jean was to write me: "I remember well the first night we met you. The two of you seemed to tumble into our little house with happiness. Hugh in love was a different Hugh, boyish and buoyant. He was so enchanted with you. And we were so enchanted with both of you. And we talked and talked (I guess we always did do that). And the two of you slept (or did not sleep) on that tiny fold-down couch that wouldn't really fit *one* tall person.

"I remember being startled when you told me that you used Johnson and Johnson's baby powder—because Hugh liked it.

And when you both left the next day Walter and I were still in the afterglow of Hugh's happiness, your happiness, and our joy that Hugh had met and married such a marvelous girl THAT WE LIKED! How young we all were . . ."

We made our way back to New York, caught up with city friends, and bought a double bed which was also extra-length, a necessity for two such tall people. We took off for northwestern Connecticut, where I had to be "shown" to old friends of Hugh's. They were theatre people who had inherited some money and retired, very young, to the country, to have children and live a simpler life than that of city and theatre. Hugh had often spent weekends with them, usually invited to meet a young woman they had picked out for him. And lo and behold, he called to say he was coming with his wife, someone they had never even heard of.

That was the weekend we bought Crosswicks, surely a rash act, but one we have never regretted. Herb and Martha were so friendly that I felt quickly at home. I told them that I'd spent many childhood summers at camp in Norfolk, just fourteen miles away, and that I loved this particular corner of the planet. Suddenly Herb said, "I think we've found a house for you," and we got in the car and drove a few miles to a back road which met a dirt road. On the corner was an old white farmhouse that looked as though it was about to fall down, largely because of a decrepit porch which had been tacked on. Herb knew enough about houses to reassure us that the basic house underneath all the disrepair was solid.

We returned to New York, and then set off for a summer of stock. Hugh was the leading man, and after the first couple of shows I was given the opportunity for some rich character roles. We stayed with friends of the producers, who had extra rooms because their three children were off at summer camp. I remember two things particularly. Our hostess said, "The telephone is for one purpose only, to let your family know if you're going to be late." Good advice, still taken to heart when I told Léna the "rules."

The other thing I remember is my first shower. It was hard to believe that I had never before in my life taken a shower! But I had always lived in places with tubs. Crosswicks had a tub, not a shower. So I washed my hair under the shower, not realizing that shower curtains must be tucked inside, until our hostess rushed up the stairs to tell me I was causing a flood.

Hugh left before the last two weeks of the season to go to the prestigious East Hampton Theatre to star in *Dangerous Corner*. I stayed on for two of my best roles of the summer. I wrote in my journal how much I missed him, adding: "But the wonderful thing, whether we are together or apart, is to know that he is in the world, and that we belong together. And what I must learn is to love with all of me, giving all of me, and yet remain whole in myself. Any other kind of love is too demanding of the other; it takes, rather than gives. To love so completely that you lose yourself in another person is not good. You are giving a weight, not the sense of lightness and light that loving someone should give. To love wholly, generously, and yet retain the core that makes you you."

Hugh stayed on an extra week at East Hampton to play the doctor in *Our Town*, while Thornton Wilder himself played the stage manager. I was able to join Hugh there and after the show we would go out to supper with Thornton Wilder, who talked about existentialism. Sometimes we were joined by Philip Barry, and producer Joshua Logan, and I learned more about the theatre as well as existentialism.

And I copied out these unidentified words: "In the face of such shape and weight of present misfortune, the voice of the individual artist may seem perhaps of no more consequence than the whirring of a cricket in the grass, but the arts do live continuously, and they live literally by faith; their names and their shapes and their uses and their basic meanings survive unchanged in all that matters through times of interruption, diminishment, neglect; they outlive governments and creeds and societies, even the very civilizations that produced them. They cannot be destroyed altogether because they represent the substance of faith, and the only reality. They are what we find when the ruins are cleared away. And even the smallest and most incomplete offering at this time can be a proud act in defense of that faith."

In all ways I was struggling to articulate reality.

Our surroundings were not yet as unreal as they were to become. In the world of the theatre we touched on reality itself, and were shocked as the world around us seemed to reach out for the unreal. Planned obsolescence was just coming in, objects made with less than excellence, built to destroy themselves or to wear out. Plastic and synthetics were just becoming available to the public. The word *synthetics* is enough: *unreal.*

Today we live in a society that seems to be less and less concerned with reality. We drink instant coffee and reconstituted orange juice. We buy our vegetables on cardboard trays covered with plastic. But perhaps the most dehumanizing thing of all is that we have allowed the media to call us consumers—ugly. No! I don't want to be a consumer. Anger consumes. Forest fires consume. Cancer consumes.

Four

The doctors and nurses in the hospital where my husband is being cared for are fighting a disease which would consume him without their skill. They are not consumers; they are trying to be nourishers, healers. We are very fortunate that there is such an excellent small hospital less than a dozen miles from Crosswicks, a well-endowed hospital which has attracted fine physicians. This northwest corner of our state, in the Litchfield hills, is a beautiful place in which to bring up a family. We have excellent medical care close at hand. My doctor daughter-in-law has hand-picked Hugh's team. We know that he is getting the best care possible.

Even so, I am grateful to have had my friend Ed's reinforcement that Hugh is receiving the state-of-the-art treatment, because the platinum chemotherapy is terribly hard on him. He is having every toxic reaction imaginable, and a few nobody thought of. First is the distressing but expected nausea.

When this lets up we bring him home to recuperate before the next round of platinum. He is terribly weak. Bion and Laurie almost have to carry him up the three steps into the kitchen. We sit him in the big comfortable chair where he can watch the bird feeder. And he sits there, staring at something we cannot see. But our hope is that the home environment will help, that home-cooked food will encourage the appetite which the platinum has destroyed.

In the evening Bion helps him up the stairs and we put him to bed, and he sighs with thankfulness to be in his own room, his own bed.

But I am uneasy about him all night, uneasy about him the next day. Again he sits in the big chair in the kitchen, looking across the fields to the woods and then the hills. His great blue eyes have a strange, unfamiliar expression. My anxiety deepens, but there is nothing specific to pin it on, just a feeling of wrongness. And surely the cancer itself is wrong enough.

In the afternoon I cross the big north field to the far corner where we are planting twenty-eight small white pines. Someone has bought the six-tenths of an acre just beyond this field, and all its trees, which have been a wildlife corridor, have been cut down to make room for a house. We have already planted poplars (they grow quickly), willows, maples, to make another wooded place for the deer and pheasant and other friendly wild creatures—and to protect our view. Last weekend, young friends came and helped dig twenty-eight holes, and three of the pines were properly planted. All the rest have to be released from the canvas ball, and then have the dirt tamped in around them. I go to work, ending up covered with mud. Because of the heavy spring rains, the ground is still very wet. I would like to cry, but only a few tears come.

At dinner Hugh barely nibbles at his food. We sit at the table for a while, talking by candlelight. Then Hugh says that he is ready for bed. He stands up, takes three steps, and drops like a felled oak.

It happens shockingly suddenly. "Oh, God," I say, and try to break his fall, but cannot. "Oh, God," the eternal cry in time of trouble.

Our doctor daughter-in-law is quick with her stethoscope, her sure fingers on his thready and irregular pulse. Hugh is conscious now, but very weak. Our son calls the fire department for the ambulance. The weekly meeting of the volunteer fire-department members is just ending, and within minutes the ambulance and four of the volunteers are at our house.

It is good to be part of a small community. Hugh is given a quick cardiogram, then put in the ambulance, and those who go with him are gentle, and ease his fear at this unexpected blow. Laurie and I follow by car, while Bion stays home to hold the fort, to answer the telephone. We do not speak much during the drive. We don't need to. I pray, the words a deep, interior rhythm.

Michael, Hugh's oncologist, is at the emergency room to meet us. The cardiologist is called in. There is genuine concern by doctors and nurses as well as immediate competence. Michael presses my shoulder in compassion.

We are allowed to stay with Hugh until all the tests are finished. He whispers, "I don't want to stay in the hospital." But there is no choice. Laurie and I wait beside the stretcher and walk with him to the elevator as he is wheeled to the cardiac care unit.

After a few days in CCU, Hugh's heart steadies, and he is moved to a private room (yet another picture), seems to be doing well, hopes to be released from the hospital. And then internal bleeding is discovered. Despite medication to prevent this very thing, he has developed three bleeding peptic ulcers and needs two transfusions. There is a heavy candida fungus on the esophagus, making it difficult for him to swallow. He is near tears. So am I.

Yet the times of emergency, of acute anxiety, are in a way

easier than the long days when nothing changes, while Hugh remains desperately ill, unable to eat, barely able to stand without a nurse on either side.

Everything is being done for him that can be done. Daily I need to remind myself that Ed said this is what he would do for his own father; it is not unrealistic to hope for a cure. Otherwise, I might not be able to hang on to the belief that this is what is best for Hugh.

There is nothing that I, personally, can do, except be there. At my family's suggestion I begin taking my little six-pound electronic typewriter with me so that I can write while Hugh is napping. This helps. For, like most of us, I feel frustrated when a situation arises where I am totally helpless, where there is nothing I can do to make anything better. I can, I hope, help Hugh a little by my presence, by the touch of my hand. But there is nothing specifically for me to do. And I think of a friend who has a coffee mug with the inscription: DON'T JUST DO SOME-THING. STAND THERE.

It is no small feat for me this summer just to stand there. To treasure the moments of beauty. Bion, Laurie, and I took the dogs last night after dinner and walked the mile-long dirt road on which Crosswicks faces. Never have I seen the sunset more glorious, the sunset at eight-thirty as June moves toward the longest days of the year. I look at my son and daughter-in-law with a deep surging of gratitude as they are walking through this summer with us.

Sometimes I walk the lane alone. Sometimes I cry. Sometimes I pray like a child and that is all right. Jesus called us to be children. Mostly I hold on to the ancient Jesus prayer, like a shipwrecked sailor clinging to the rope that keeps him from sinking into the deep.

I have to watch out for echthroid projections, those horrible temptations to the imagination to project terrible things, nasty little temptations which buzz around like mosquitoes.

Take it day by day. Don't project. Stand there.

* One of my experiences in standing there came after our return from summer theatre—that first year of our marriage. I had talked about wanting to wait two years before thinking about a baby, but Hugh's impetuousness infected me. And once again I was reminded of the precariousness of our lives.

Hugh and Don, an actor friend, were driving back to New York after the closing of the East Hampton season. They were both eager to get home, and were driving along considerably above the speed limit. It was still warm, and the windows were open, and suddenly a large bee flew in and started buzzing at them. They tried to shoo it out, and it outwitted them. Hugh, who was driving, slowed the car down, and further down, as the bee kept buzzing. Just as he had the car slowed to perhaps twenty miles an hour, the right front tire blew.

Had they been going faster, it is quite likely they would have been killed. Don, who was a Scotsman, believed firmly that the bee had been sent to save their lives.

Hugh got safely home, and this near-brush with death made postponements of any part of our life undesirable. Soon after that, I became pregnant, and we were delighted. It never occurred to me that I would have any problem with pregnancy, but I was, it seemed, allergic to my own little one, and the eminent obstetrician, overburdened with a multitude of postwar pregnancies, was not particularly interested. I went to Dr. Baumstone, the gentle physician who had been so helpful to Hugh after the albumin had been discovered in his urine. He noticed a slight redness in my eyes, and sent me to an ophthalmologist, Dr. Townley Paton, who was to start the Eye Bank. He immediately put me in the hospital and may well have kept me from losing the baby.

The treatment for iritis in those days included completely resting the eyes: no reading, no writing. When I was a child the most terrible punishment my mother could give me was to forbid me to read or write for twenty-four hours, and I would beg her to spank me instead. So this was a terrible deprivation. I could play the piano for a little while. But mostly, after I was out of the hospital, I lay on the couch. And my young new husband was patient and tender and gentle. He went out on a nasty, rainy day and came back with a small basket of strawberries. Pregnant women are supposed to have a craving for strawberries. Not I. Much as I wanted to eat them in appreciation of his thoughtfulness, I couldn't. But Hugh stood there with me for the first five months of misery.

Mother sent us this poem from a newspaper and I copied it in my journal—I did cheat a little on resting the eyes by writing for a few minutes each day:

> *To keep one sacred flame*
> *Through life, unchilled, unmoved,*
> *To love in wintry age the same*
> *As first in youth we loved,*
> *To feel that we adore*
> *Even to fond excess,*
> *That though the heart would break with more*
> *It could not live with less.*

* * *

❧ I understand that poem better this summer of Hugh's illness than forty years earlier when I copied it out.

But already I was beginning to glimpse that kind of love.

If the first five months of my pregnancy tested all of Hugh's patience and love, the remainder of the time was happy. The baby was an active little thing; all I needed to do in bed at night was curl around Hugh and she would start kicking him, emphasizing that this new life belonged to both of us.

My energy returned as all the various side effects of the pregnancy left me. I was allowed to use my eyes to read and write. We went out to dinner, had friends in. One evening it was the people from the Theatre Guild, Very Important People, and I was determined to do Hugh proud. I cooked a good dinner, because I am a good cook—up to dessert. For dessert I had made one of Hugh's favorites, a deep-dish cherry pie. When it came time to serve it, the crust did not look brown enough, so I put it under the broiler.

Hugh had to get the fire extinguisher to put out the blaze.

Despite my total discomfiture, I doubt if it did his career any harm.

One morning he received a phone call from Margaret Webster, asking if he could sing.

Peggy was directing a new production of *Alice in Wonderland*, with herself playing the Red Queen, and Eva Le Gallienne the White. The man playing the White Knight had broken his arm, and they needed a replacement.

But Hugh told Peggy he couldn't sing, and hung up.

I had very carefully observed a policy of non-interference.

Hugh had recently closed in Pirandello's *Henry V*. Nothing else was on the horizon. I knew that he had a lovely voice. I called Peggy Webster. "If you mean can Hugh sing in the Metropolitan Opera, no. But if you mean can he put over a song, yes."

So he auditioned and was hired. Worked with the pianist on the White Knight's solo, which was syncopated, modulated, and difficult, and had to be sung after he had fallen off a horse three times. The horse was two tall men standing upright under the frame. Hugh was taught to fall correctly, warned against breaking his arm. On the evening when he went on as the White Knight he was singing with the orchestra for the first time. Of course I was in the audience, visibly pregnant, and all our friends in the company were rather nervous that I might have the baby that night.

I didn't, and Hugh was good, if a little breathless. His costume was countless pieces of armor, not light in weight, and included a half face mask with a long, drooping nose to match the drooping mustache. As the weeks turned toward spring, and then summer, and the heat increased, he began to perspire in the heavy armor, and drops of sweat fell off his own aristocratic nose into the false one and began to back up. Holes had to be made in the White Knight's nose so that Hugh didn't drown in his own sweat.

It was a lovely production and I thought slightly wistfully that had I not been pregnant I might well have played one of the minor roles. An album of the show was made, on the old breakable 78 rpm records, and is a great treasure.

One night after the show we met an agent for supper and her guest was John Gielgud. I wrote in my journal that a few years earlier I would have been overwhelmed with awe to the point of speechlessness. While I was honored to meet this famous actor, I was amazingly comfortable and relaxed enough to enjoy his conversation, and relieved that in person he was as delightful as he was onstage.

***

&. We enjoyed intimate groups far more than we did the enormous bashes we were sometimes expected to attend, where we had the feeling that whoever was talking to us was looking past our shoulders to see if there was someone more important across the room, and the decibel level rose so high that real conversation was not possible. Our idea of a pleasant evening was a small group of people eating a well-cooked meal together, and talking about art and the world and life and the theatre and what it was to try to be human and all the many topics of conversation that make for a creative and stimulating evening.

The cutthroat theatre world that I have read about in novels was probably there, but it is a world that has to be chosen, and one we did not wish to choose.

***

&. We saw old friends, made new ones, such as Arthur and Ruth Farmer, with whom we "clicked" immediately. Arthur was a copyright lawyer and knew everyone in publishing, so we had a good many friends in common. He was also an amateur violinist, and he and Ruth had an outstanding collection of records, and we spent many evenings talking and listening and talking.

We watched Anne Jackson's romance and ultimate marriage to Eli Wallach, reliving, in a way, our own days of courtship. We saw Walter and Jean Kerr, and I'll never forget Jean saying, "I've just discovered cake mixes! It makes me feel rather wicked, sort of like artificial insemination." And of course we continued to see Thelma, who was stage manager for *Alice*, and Cavada and others from the *Cherry Orchard* company.

We were living life as fully as possible. No postponements.

🍂 Josephine was born on the twenty-eighth of June, the same day as the last performance of *Alice in Wonderland*. Thelma remarked, "We can always remember the day that *Alice* closed, because it was the day that Madeleine opened."

It was not an easy birth. Hugh, of course, had to be at the theatre. He brought me to the hospital in the small hours of the morning on Saturday, a matinee day. Even had it not been, he would not have been allowed to be with me. Nor was my mother, who had come North for the big event. I spent hours alone, during a long labor, in a hospital full of that first postwar crop of babies. The obstetrician, who had not seemed particularly interested during my pregnancy, did not seem interested in the delivery. Every once in a while a nurse would come in and say, "Push."

Ultimately I was wheeled into the delivery room, a cone of ether slapped on my face, and the baby removed with forceps. Fortunately there were no ill effects. Josephine was a beautiful baby. But the treatment by nurses and doctor had been humiliating. I looked at this tiny, perfect creature and felt nothing other than an aesthetic pleasure that Hugh's and my collaboration had been so successful. I am grateful indeed that I insisted on nursing my baby, and I had to insist, to make a fuss. I was urged not to. Women didn't nurse in those days; it wasn't scientific; a bottle of formula every four hours was what was recommended. Something stubborn in me made me fight for the right to do what seemed to me to be natural.

So Josephine was brought in, put to my breast, and it was as though a light switch had been turned on. A great rush of love, mother love, flooded out of me as my child, my very own infant, began to suck.

At one feeding time the baby was brought in to me and I started to put her to my breast and felt something wrong. The ears weren't right. I looked at the blue-and-white bracelet and rang the bell. "This isn't my baby!" A good thing that immediate identification of babies was now standard.

Josephine thrived on my milk and the head nurse on the floor told me that one feeding was going to be cut out, the 2 a.m. feeding.

I said firmly, "My husband is an actor. We're up at 2 a.m. We'll cut the 6 a.m. feeding."

This was neither hospital procedure nor policy. But I had won the battle to nurse my baby in the first place. I was going to win the battle to nurse her on Hugh's and my hours, not the hospital's. "It's my milk," I announced, "and my baby. If you bring her in to me at 6 a.m. I'm turning my breasts to the wall."

This was not a spur-of-the-moment decision. As my policy was to get decently dressed as soon as I got up in the morning, so it seemed to me only good sense to put the baby on our hours. I had seen other theatre wives doing what was then customary: getting up to feed the baby at six in the morning and then either being asleep when their husbands got home from the theatre or being exhausted and bedraggled. Why should a husband come home to a sleeping wife? Why not go out and have supper with someone else? I wanted Hugh home with the baby and me.

In the South it is the custom for the grandmother to provide a baby nurse for the first six weeks, and my mother wanted to follow this custom. She was not strong enough to do much herself, and she wanted to make sure I didn't get too exhausted.

We had made friends with a practical nurse who walked her dog at the same time we walked Touché. She had a friend who was a baby nurse, and who would be free a week after we brought Josephine home from the hospital. That worked out well. Mother returned to the South. Hugh went off for three weeks to do a play—*Hedda Gabler*—at a good theatre in Maine. And Johanna moved in.

Johanna wore a white nurse's uniform and cap and was forceful and competent. She was concerned about me. Despite the fact that I was nursing the baby, I was bleeding more than she thought normal. My energy level was low. She called the obstetrician, who was busy and disinterested. Johanna had a friend, a doctor, whom she called by his last name—Nedelsohn. Nedelsohn, too, was concerned: he gave me a shot of Ergotrate, of vitamins.

There was something about Nedelsohn that made me want to draw back. But what was I to do? My mother was in Florida, my husband in Maine. I was alone with the baby and Johanna and Nedelsohn. I had to trust them. And it was true. I had no energy. I was still bleeding profusely. Johanna made thick eggnogs for me, but I was not hungry. The weeks of Hugh's absence dragged on and I did not improve. Johanna felt that when he returned, when he was beside me in bed at night, I would be better. She called the doctor twice more. She was a registered nurse but he did not take her seriously.

Later I was to write: "Monday morning Hugh came back. I was still half asleep as he came rushing into the bedroom and we tumbled into each other's arms. I was so happy to have him home and we spent a beautiful morning admiring the baby and just being happy until Hugh and Johanna decided I had to have a nap.

"While I was sleeping Arthur Farmer called. They had an

explosion at their place in the country and Ruth was burned and died. Of course we were terribly depressed by that, and so terribly sorry for Arthur—he and Ruth were so happy together and so right for each other and it was such a ghastly painful way for Ruth to die."

Johanna talked us into going out for dinner and we went down the street to Enrico and Paglieri's. Then we went home and Johanna went out with Nedelsohn. She didn't get home till almost midnight, by which time we were just about ready for bed. Hugh went into the bathroom to wash, and I stayed in the living room talking to Johanna about Hugh—how he had lost weight and what I should do to make him gain. He called out in a sleepy voice that he was through in the bathroom. I said I'd be there in a minute. I felt that I was bleeding a bit and was just about to say, "Good Lord, haven't I finished bleeding yet!" when all of a sudden the blood began to gush out of me, all over my nightgown, my robe, the chair, the floor, pouring out of me in great spurts. I cried, "I'm bleeding like mad!" Johanna looked, and went whipping into the bedroom for cotton, which she stuffed between my legs, telling me not to move.

I was terrified. I had never seen so much blood before and it was horribly frightening to see it flooding out of me. Johanna called the obstetrician and gave him quick hell and got his permission to give me a shot of Ergotrate, which she fortunately had. She said she did not dare move me from the chair until something slowed the blood down. Thank God she was there when it happened. She was wonderful about reassuring me. She gave me the Ergotrate, then pulled out the couch and got me down on that. The blood was still coming out but no longer so violently. She called Nedelsohn to see if she should give me more Ergotrate, but he said not so soon. He said he would be down with more in case my doctor didn't bring any. He didn't.

There wasn't time to wait for an ambulance, so I was driven to the hospital in a car, Nedelsohn's or the obstetrician's—I'm not sure which. It wasn't the hospital where Josephine was born ("He was ashamed to go back there," Johanna said of the obstetrician), but uptown, Women's Hospital. Hugh came with me. Johanna stayed with the baby. In the car on the way up the West Side I kept thinking of Ruth Farmer—Ruth, who wasn't much older than I, and who was dead.

I was barely allowed to tell Hugh I loved him, have him say he loved me, kiss me, before I was whisked off to the operating room. The obstetrician had left inside me a goodly portion of placenta. No wonder I was bleeding too much. No wonder I had no energy.

The result of this—what I can only call carelessness—was that I had childbed fever. Antibiotics were just coming in. My chills and fever were treated with penicillin, which was then being used only when it was a matter of life and death.

I don't remember how long I was in the hospital, separated from my baby. A month or more. My milk dried up. The obstetrician now came every day. So did Nedelsohn. The obstetrician said I needed one thing, Nedelsohn the opposite. Hugh and I felt caught in a trap. We were dependent on Johanna to take care of the baby, which she did with love and skill. But with Johanna came Nedelsohn. She had brought him in because of her concern for me, but we felt that his continuing presence was not appropriate. Johanna did not try to conceal the fact that they were lovers. She had absolute faith in his skill as a doctor, and none in the obstetrician's—with a certain amount of justice.

Hugh paid a visit to Dr. Baumstone to tell him of our predicament. Whom were we to trust?

Dr. Baumstone listened with concern as Hugh told him what

the obstetrician advised, what Nedelsohn advised, shook his head and finally said that he thought Nedelsohn was right.

The problem was that we did not trust him. There was something about him that made us terribly uncomfortable. He seemed obsessed with sex to the point of perversity. One time he went into the bathroom of my hospital room and I confided to Hugh later that I thought he was using my toothbrush, and Hugh took that suspicion seriously, so weird did Nedelsohn seem to us.

Ultimately I was released from the hospital. Johanna was not only willing to stay on to help with the baby, she insisted. And I felt too weak and exhausted and depressed to say no. Not only was I devoid of energy, but the childbed fever or the antibiotic or both had left me with a profound depression. I felt as though I were imprisoned behind a sheet of frozen glass with everybody else on the other side; I could not thaw it enough to get through.

Finally I felt well enough to tell Johanna that it was time for her to go, that Hugh and I needed our own lives with our baby. I was grateful to her; she had probably saved my life with her quick action and her Ergotrate when I hemorrhaged. If we could have had Johanna for a few more weeks without Nedelsohn, we might have considered it. But Nedelsohn, despite the fact that he was probably a very good physician, gave us the creeps.

As for the obstetrician, I did not see him again. Hugh and I are not litigious people, but surely we had a case against this expensive specialist. I wrote him a letter, which Arthur Farmer, our lawyer as well as friend, checked and passed. I told the doctor that I was sending him a check for one-third of his bill. He had not cared for me properly during my pregnancy, or during the postpartum days, despite Johanna's warnings. But I had a beautiful baby, so I was sending him a third of what he charged. He accepted the check.

A few months later we learned that our suspicions of Nedelsohn were not unfounded. From our dog-walking nurse friend we learned that Nedelsohn had killed himself because he had been exposed as part of a drug ring. That same day Johanna called to tell us that Nedelsohn had had a heart attack and died. We were shocked but somehow not surprised and what we felt was mostly terrible pity for Johanna.

At last I had pushed through the frozen glass between the world and me, and was able to rejoice in our child, in my husband and our love. I wrote, "This winter for the first time I have felt beautiful. It is a good feeling and I am glad for Hugh's sake and also (and most important) because it frees me to think less about myself and more about other people. I am surer of myself. I know that I look well, so I don't have to worry about it, or feel self-conscious, and I can give more to other people.

"At last, at last I have thrown off the shadow of the illness after Jo's birth. The wounds have all healed and only the neat scar remains and it is endurable. And at last I am in love with life again—just the simple, ordinary things that can suddenly seem so beautiful and so exciting—seeing a small curve of moon between the buildings, pouring out a glass of milk, seeing Jo smile, pulling a book out of the bookcase, saying hello to the butcher and having him smile at me, just smiling at anyone in the street, feeling Jo's arms go about my neck, feeling Hugh's arms go about me in his sleep."

The pattern of our lives once again became ours. Hugh worked in a number of early television shows, such as the Pulitzer Prize Playhouse. When he got a good role in another play and left for the theatre in the evening, I would put Josephine in her crib and go to the typewriter. When Hugh came home, we woke the baby and brought her into the living room with us, so that we could have our evening together as a family. When we went to bed around 2 a.m., we put her back in her crib, and when we woke up in the morning we reached into the crib and pulled her out and into bed with us. The touch of her small and perfect body against ours was a wonderful affirmation.

Five

We need affirmation this summer. I spend much of the day at the hospital, trying to be there before lunch is brought in, to stay until after supper, in order to encourage Hugh to eat. He is going through a bad time in all ways. It is hard to keep a sense of proportion, a sense of humor, and yet I know that laughter is most necessary when things are difficult. Life on this planet in general is not very humorous. There is nothing funny about the disaster of the *Challenger*, or about Chernobyl, or the cutting down of the rain forests. There is nothing funny about cancer. But despite all the horror and tragedy there is still the possibility of genuine laughter. One of Hugh's favorite stories of the summer is that of a friend anxiously calling Bion when Hugh was first in the hospital and asking, "Have you got the results of the autopsy yet?" and then catching himself and saying, "Oh, that's not what I meant . . ."

Or a nurse saying to Hugh, "You mean you look like the man who played Dr. Tyler on television?"

"No, I *am* the man who played Dr. Tyler."

At which the overcome nurse could only gasp, "Oh, wow, I don't believe it!"

Or watching the puppies (golden retrievers are still puppies at nearly three) tear across the field to the haying machine, which had been left as our neighboring farmer broke for lunch, come to a sudden halt as they think better of the red monster, and gallop back to us and safety.

Or seeing an eighteen-month-old grandson (when Maria and John come for a quick visit before the new baby is born) wave a hand and call out, "Hiya!"

I do not want ever to be indifferent to the joys and beauties of this life. For through these, as through pain, we are enabled to see purpose in randomness, pattern in chaos. We do not have to understand in order to believe that behind the mystery and the fascination there is love.

In the midst of what we are going through this summer I have to hold on to this, to return to the eternal questions without demanding an answer. The questions worth asking are not answerable. Could we be fascinated by a Maker who was completely explained and understood? The mystery is tremendous, and the fascination that keeps me returning to the questions affirms that they are worth asking, and that any God worth believing in is the God not only of the immensities of the galaxies I rejoice in at night when I walk the dogs, but also the God of love who cares about the sufferings of us human beings and is here, with us, for us, in our pain and in our joy.

I come across four lines of Yeats and copy them down:

> But Love has pitched her mansion in
> The place of excrement;
> For nothing can be sole or whole
> That has not been rent.

The place of excrement. That is where we are this summer. How do we walk through excrement and keep clean in the heart? How do we become whole by being rent?

This summer is not the first time I have walked through the place of excrement and found love's mansion there. Indeed, we are more likely to find it in the place of excrement than in the sterile places. God comes where there is pain and brokenness, waiting to heal, even if the healing is not the physical one we hope for.

Hugh has one setback after another. He cannot eat. He loses forty pounds and he was thin to start with. Just as he begins to try walking up and down the hospital corridor, he is hit with an acute attack of gout in his left foot, and even though this is not an uncommon response of the body to the indignity of surgery, I am outraged.

I leave him for two days to keep my promise to be with my friend Luci Shaw at a convention of Christian booksellers. During my brief time at the Convention Center in Washington I hear different people tell of some good or lucky event and then say, "Surely the Lord was with me." And my hackles rise. My husband is desperately ill, so where is the Lord? What about that place of excrement? Isn't that where Love's mansion is pitched? Isn't that where God is?

Doesn't such an attitude trivialize the activities and concerns of the Maker? Doesn't it imply that God is with us only during the good and fortuitous times and withdraws or abandons us when things go wrong?

I will have nothing to do with a God who cares only occasionally. I need a God who is with us always, everywhere, in the deepest depths as well as the highest heights. It is when things go wrong, when the good things do not happen, when our prayers seem to have been lost, that God is most present. We do not need the sheltering wings when things go smoothly. We are closest to God in the darkness, stumbling along blindly.

Yet even here I live with contradiction. Whenever anyone in the family is driving, I pray for a safe journey. And when I hear the car door slam and know that whoever it is is safely home, I breathe out, "Oh, God, thank you."

But I think there is a difference between offering a deep sigh of thanks and assuming that "the Lord was surely with me."

We need to say "Thank you" whenever possible, even if we are not able to reconcile the human creature's free will with the Maker's working out of the pattern. Thanks and praise are, I believe, some of the threads with which the pattern is woven.

There are many times when the idea that there is indeed a pattern seems absurd wishful thinking. Random events abound. There is much in life that seems meaningless. And then, when I can see no evidence of meaning, some glimpse is given which reveals the strange weaving of purposefulness and beauty.

The world of science lives fairly comfortably with paradox. We know that light is a wave, and also that light is a particle. The discoveries made in the infinitely small world of particle physics indicate randomness and chance, and I do not find it any more difficult to live with the paradox of a universe of randomness and chance and a universe of pattern and purpose than I do with light as a wave and light as a particle. Living with contradiction is nothing new to the human being.

☙ After a month in the hospital Hugh comes home, as thin as though he'd just been released from concentration camp.

He is unable to eat, barely able to walk, he is still so weak. But he is happy to be home, among familiar things, looking out the windows to the peace of the view across the freshly hayed fields—it looks as though we have ten acres of lawn! Beyond the fields are the woods, and beyond the woods the Litchfield hills. Hugh sits in the big chair in the kitchen and turns from the view to the birds crowding around the feeder—the purple and house finches, the downy woodpecker, the brilliant cardinals, all putting on a show for him. Usually in the summer we move the feeders off the terrace and into the trees, filling them only occasionally, but this summer they are there for Hugh's pleasure. Simply watching them takes all his energy, though sometimes he manages to knock on the window with his cane to scare away the greedy mourning doves so that they won't take the food away from the smaller birds.

One day he shows us a letter from Texas with the address on *Morn*ing Dove Drive, managing a smile as he shows us the changed spelling. On rainy days he points out the bedraggledness of the female cardinals, their elegant crested "hats" floppily askew. We rejoice at each small sign of interest, for nothing more can be done to treat him, either by chemotherapy or by surgery, until he has regained some appetite and a little strength. At this moment anything more would kill him outright.

The oncologist goes away with his family for a week's vacation. When he sees Hugh on his return he says openly, "He looks terrible." He does. It is hard for me to understand that it is still possible that all this is reversible. I show the doctor a snapshot of Hugh taken not long ago, saying, "In case you've forgotten, this is what he really looks like. This is the man I want back."

Even at home the fungus on the esophagus and the three ulcers make it almost impossible for him to eat. He lives on a fortified drink three times a day which we make palatable by putting it in the blender with ice cream. Hugh has not had ice cream in nearly two decades. "Forget the diabetic diet," we are told. "Give him anything he can eat. He has got to have some nourishment."

These are rough days. We know that Hugh has to eat, to walk, to gain strength. But he cannot eat. He has absolutely no appetite. Nothing tastes as it should. It is possible that yet another side effect of the platinum is that it has done something to his taste buds.

Meals are horrors. We know that we must try to live—for ourselves, for Hugh—as normally as possible. Bion and Laurie and I promise each other that we won't push Hugh to eat, that if he doesn't want food we won't say anything. But we can't keep our promise. We can't keep from urging Hugh to eat, in our longing to help. We struggle to create meals of what we call "slippery" food, and nothing seems to work.

One day when Carol is here, helping me clean the house, I urge Hugh to come with me for his morning walk, and he refuses. When I keep on urging, he shouts, "No!"

Later Carol told me that Hugh said to her, "You're upset because I yelled at Madeleine, aren't you?"

She replied, "Yes. It's only because she loves you that she wants you to walk."

And Hugh says, "I know." Oh, I know that he knows.

With my head I know that he has to work out anger, and that I am the "safe" person to take it out on. Head and heart do not always work together.

Not for any of us. We get impatient. We think Hugh could be trying harder. We do not understand the magnitude of all that he is working through, nor that the inability to eat is in no way his "fault," is not in his control.

This is a bad, bad time, with no one, not even the doctors, aware of just how badly Hugh's body is betraying him.

We must not run into false guilt over all this. In our own fumbling, totally human ways we are doing the best that we can.

It is not good enough. But we are not saints or angels, but ordinary people fumbling to love, falling over our own helplessness and frustration.

And Hugh is trying—trying to eat, and not succeeding. Going with me, now, for a walk each day. Trying to swim. He works up to ten laps in the small pool, diligently, bravely. Friends send me a tape of charming French-Canadian music, *Mes quatre saisons*, and Hugh and I love it, and swim to it.

It is not good to indulge in hindsight. If we had known how sheerly physical Hugh's eating problem was, we would not have pushed so hard. How could we know? Even the gastroenterologist had no idea of what a terrible state the esophagus was in.

Hugh has to work through all the anguish and frustration and denial and acceptance himself. The lonely valley is just that: lonely. Jesus walked that lonesome valley. He had to walk it by himself. Sooner or later we all do. There are no shortcuts through the place of excrement.

The constant strain is wearing on us all. We are tired. I admit that I am stressed—no difficult admission. And it occurs to me that if stressed means all strung out, tense, worn, then distressed should mean the opposite. But it doesn't. I am both stressed and distressed. Held together by the love of family and friends.

A letter comes which tells of a time when someone in the writer's family was desperately ill, and she found that during this time of terrible anxiety she noticed small, lovely things far more than when life went on in its more ordinary way. And that is true, a strange gift born of pain. I am poignantly aware of the glory of the fair-weather clouds constantly moving in the blue summer sky; of the deliciousness of food, especially the fresh vegetables as we bring them in from the garden; the softness of newly washed sheets.

But anxiety is never far below the surface. Once he has taken a short walk or had his swim, Hugh does little except read the paper and do the puzzle. He seems to be far away from us. Every once in a while he returns with a smile or a quick and witty remark and for a moment he is back with us; he is himself.

Once I sit at his feet, perching on his footstool. I say, "Darling, we've always promised to be absolutely honest with each other, and I don't think we are, right now. I'm very angry at everything that has happened. It isn't fair. It shouldn't have happened. You've got to be angry, too."

He acknowledges this, and we hold each other. Cry.

To accept that we are angry is a healthy and appropriate response as long as we don't get stuck in it. Acknowledging it is one way of going through it. Hugh has to go through it his own way.

It is hard to have him so far away.

Six

Sometimes Hugh's farawayness has been literal; physical, not spiritual.

If my childhood and young womanhood were not typical of the usual pattern of growing up in America, neither was my marriage. Hugh had to take jobs as they came. Sometimes he would go out of town with the tryout of a play that never made it to Broadway. Even if it did, we never knew how long it was going to run. When he got an out-of-town job he had to take it. Separation is a normal part of a theatrical marriage.

My second novel had been published to distinguished reviews but very modest sales, and I was running out of *The Small Rain* money. And we now had a baby to support, blessed in having a child who was healthy and happy and full of fun. Hugh would hold out his forefingers and she would clasp them and he would swing her, lifting her high, to my mother's terror when she came to visit.

Television was in its early days, all live, and often exhausting. When Hugh played the John Barrymore role in *The Royal Family* he had to carry Florence Reed, a hefty actress, up a flight of stairs. On the day of the performance, rehearsals started in the early morning, and before the show went on the air that evening he had carried Florence Reed up those stairs twenty times. When he came home, he was so worn out that he threw up. Such was the glamorous world of the theatre.

But it was our life and I married Hugh with no illusions of stability. We managed and we were happy.

๛ Happy with our child. Josephine had her first birthday at Crosswicks, took her first steps, began running all over in delight. Eva Le Gallienne sent her the little nursery chair that had been used in *The Cherry Orchard* and she carried it everywhere, using it as a stepladder. It took the place of the more usual blanket or stuffed toy.

We spent nearly six months in our run-down house, scrubbing, cleaning, painting. In those days of frequent trains I could drive Hugh down to the early-morning train at West Cornwall, and he could easily get to the city. After the train had pulled out I drove along a dirt road by the Housatonic River to Don Cameron's for breakfast and talk. Don was an older actor from the Civic Repertory who had been introduced to me by Thelma. He was friend, father-figure, mentor. I never heard him say a mean or sarcastic word about anybody. He was realistic enough in his expectations of human relations to understand betrayal, and the complexities of human behavior, without judgment. Quietly, patiently, he taught me. Our breakfasts were a treasured part of that summer.

Hugh was away a good deal at various summer-stock theatres, so I spent much of the time alone with our little one. And I wrote. That was the summer I wrote *And Both Were Young*. And I learned something else about art: I knew that if the book was accepted by the publisher, if it was "good," then I would always remember the summer as a "good" summer. If it was not accepted, if it did not work, then I would remember the summer as a "bad" summer. Illogical, but true. The book was accepted with enthusiasm, and so it was a "good" summer despite Hugh's many long absences.

We bought one of the early power mowers, and it was my job to mow the lawn. During the years, as mowers were refined and did the job more easily, our lawn grew bigger until it took Hugh nearly three hours sitting on his tractor to mow what is now a couple of acres.

One afternoon during that first summer the blades struck something solid, so I pulled the mower away, stopped it, bent down, and picked up a silver napkin ring, an ancient, tarnished silver napkin ring, inscribed Jacob. It has been my napkin ring ever since.

One July day my journal entry was headed: "Social Note: Last night about one o'clock I was in bed reading when I heard a low whistle outside my window. When I heard the whistle again, I got up and looked out the window. I saw a man standing there. The man said, 'Magda!' Only my friends from *The Cherry Orchard* call me Magda. I was baffled, and called out in a whisper, 'Who is it?' 'Bob.' Of course I then went dashing downstairs in my nightclothes to let him in. 'What are you doing here!' I cried. 'We came over to see the show at Litchfield,' he told me. Then I saw that there were some people out in a car, so I said, 'Bring 'em in and I'll dash up and put some clothes on.' So we had a pleasant social half hour before they set off."

I noticed small things alone that I might not have if Hugh had not been away with a show. "The shadow of a moth as it flies about at night can look as though it came from a huge bat or bird. Quite terrifying sometimes."

When Hugh got home at the end of the summer season at Holyoke, we threw a big party for all of the company, and the ingenue (one of those "little blondes" Pepé was reputed to like) very overtly threw herself at Hugh. He was amused, not interested, and it was not the last time I watched women who were perhaps younger and certainly more beautiful than I making a play for my husband. I didn't like it, having never completely thrown off my insecurity, but Hugh had taken the marriage vows as seriously as I had, and I had no cause for worry. I never understood why a woman felt she was free to attract another woman's husband, but I did understand that I needn't be concerned. In the nature of Hugh's business, he was more often thrown with beautiful women than I, a solitary writer, was thrown with handsome men, but together we learned the meaning of faithfulness.

Hugh and I wanted more children but it did not seem wise to have a new baby when our livelihood was so totally precarious. Crosswicks, while not large, was still a farmhouse, with four bedrooms upstairs, but much of the year we had to be in New York, with one bedroom. We loved our Tenth Street apartment but it was too small for us with even one child. Apartment hunting was discouraging; apartments were few, and those we could find with two bedrooms were too expensive for us. Leonard Bernstein lived on the top floor of our building, with two small bedrooms, and we talked of switching apartments, because he didn't like the climb, but we felt that four flights of stairs wouldn't be really practical with two children, so nothing came of that idea. I wondered if our incomes would ever stabilize. We had enough money to live on, but not enough to save on, even with subletting the apartment during the summer.

Very few families yet had television sets, and some evenings when Hugh was going to be on a show in a particularly good role I would take the baby, walk up to the nearest bar, order a glass of ginger ale, and ask if I could please watch my husband. It was amazing how gently I was treated by the masculine clientele watching football or baseball. Immediately the channel would be changed, and everybody watched with me and admired Hugh.

In the spring we sublet our apartment and moved up to Crosswicks, planted our vegetable garden. I started a new novel, *Camilla*, and enjoyed writing it.

I was happy with our little girl and our house and the peace of the view across the fields to the north, and the gentle ancient shoulders of the Litchfield hills. But the world kept breaking in. On the fifteenth of June 1950, I wrote: "Today the communists marched into Korea and Harry McLeod died. To Mrs. McLeod the agony of the Koreans is as nothing compared to the witnessed agony of a frail man coughing his life out in a blank hospital room. To the world the passing of Harry McLeod is nothing; only in Goshen is anyone aware of this upright man's life and death. He ran the little grocery store in West Goshen and he gave fair measure, and running over. Harry McLeod was and now he is not. Yesterday the communists were not in Korea and now they are there, and if the passing of Harry McLeod has in the long run no profound effect on mankind, what will the occupation of Korea have? How does it affect the small, good people in Korea, the Harry McLeods? And how are we to judge it and what are we to do and how will this action, this attempt to strangle freedom, affect us and our children and our children's children?"

The effects were violent and continuous, but ordinary daily life went on, cooking meals, making beds, rocking and singing my little one to sleep.

The world broke in on me in another way, in late September. Hugh was in New York doing a Dumont television broadcast and all of our special Goshen friends wanted to see it. Eunice and Burt, old Goshen people, arranged for us to go over to one of the few houses which had a television set. Burt was a farmer, and Hugh helped him hay, driving the tractor while Burt picked up the hay. Eunice, with infinite patience, taught this city girl how to can and freeze.

I was a little nervous about the evening Eunice and Burt had set up so that we could watch Hugh. Our host was the head of the American Legion in Goshen and the leader of a group of men who were out looking for communists, immediately labeling anyone interested in the United Nations, or peace, as "Red! Red!" I was well aware that the communists were doing their best to infiltrate and destroy, but I did not believe that the people concerned about peace were the ones who were dangerous. I realized, with a feeling of terror in the pit of my stomach, that our host could actually ruin Hugh if he wanted to, by accusing him of communism, because I had seen it being done to other actors.

"Where am I living?" I wrote. "Is this a town in Germany under Hitler, or Russia under Stalin, or is it a town in the democratic country of the United States of America?"

The evening of the Dumont show came and went, but extraordinary events were happening because of the blind terror of communism. Don sent me a clipping from the *The New York Times* with the headline: "HIAWATHA MAY AID REDS, SAYS STUDIO. *Indian chief immortalized by Longfellow sought peace, so Monogram shelves film.*" This was as skewed in the opposite direction as that New Year's Eve party where I learned that communism was not for me.

I was working on my novel, and certainly my reaction to the blind terror of communism I had just witnessed was reflected as I wrote about Camilla's friend, Frank, with his passion for peace. I finished the book, and I was happy with it. Hugh, too, loved and believed in it. But Vanguard, which had published my first two novels, rejected it. I sent it off again: another rejection, but for diametrically opposite reasons. I wrote: "*How* do you reconcile such diverse opinions? I'm always much too close to my work to be able to judge it myself until several years have elapsed."

The next entry was simply: "From an Icelandic saga: Every fate is to be overcome by bearing it." The struggle to be writer, wife, mother, human being, was one I shared with many women. Even if it was not saga-like, it was mine.

Arthur Farmer read the manuscript and was enthusiastic, and I was encouraged, because I knew Arthur to be a severe critic who would make no bones about it if he didn't like something. But he saw what I was trying to do in the book, and why I wanted to do it, and said he saw no reason why Knopf wouldn't take it. Knopf had published Willa Cather. I would be more than honored to be published by Knopf. Arthur also had several perceptive criticisms, and those helped too because the early rejections had made no sense to me.

It was indeed good of Arthur to offer to show the book to Knopf. He was still deep in grief over Ruth's death. He knew personally a great many editors and publishers but he had certainly never played literary agent before. Of course he had no way of knowing when he offered to show *Camilla* that it was not going to be easy to find a publisher.

One evening when Hugh was off with a play, I wrote in my journal: "I have read and read and am still wide awake. When I am in bed with Hugh I can lie close to him, my foot touching him, or my hand against him, and be able to relax. When I am alone the night is darker and the wind less friendly. Our marriage has seemed to settle and develop this year into something much warmer and deeper. It is much more quiet, and I think this is the way it is going to have to go on growing. I must continue learning to channel my waters, my wild waters, into gentler ways."

And then, only a few days later: "So. Knopf has rejected *Camilla*. I haven't even particularly wanted to cry except for a moment when Hugh was too kind in telling me on the phone and for a few minutes afterwards—and then I conquered the feeling quite easily. The only tangible reaction I had was a tremendous and utter fatigue, a need to lie down and sleep and sleep. And even that I seem to have overcome, too.

"The telephone just rang and it was Hugh—just to talk. Very sweet of him. He can be so thoughtful and wonderful. For the record: Arthur told Hugh that he would like to show the ms. to Rinehart. They're a good house, so I said, go ahead. And it is awfully good of Arthur and I am grateful for *his* faith in the book.

"A sad thing: the kitchen floor was laid today and the new sink is all installed. The kitchen looks superb and glamorous. But because of poor rejected *Camilla*, it has lost half its glory. All is ashes, ashes . . ."

And: "Perhaps I am a real writer as long as I go on writing, as long as I go on trying, which I shall always do."

But it was not easy. The editor at Rinehart "really loved" *Camilla*, but his salesmen didn't think they could sell it. Arthur was planning to take it to Scribner's, and his unshakable faith in the book kept my own faith in it going.

And at last I wrote: "Arthur called me from New York today to tell me that Simon and Schuster is publishing *Camilla*." Oh, I was relieved! And *Camilla* ultimately has done very well: first publication as a regular trade novel, followed by two reissues as a young-adult novel, first by Crowell in the sixties, and then by Delacorte in the eighties.

I wrote: "It has been a cold, rainy day; and I still haven't been quite able to believe that Simon and Schuster is really taking

Camilla. I played Camilla's music to try to believe, Holst's *The Planets*, and Prokofiev's Third Piano Concerto. It is good to be able to allow Camilla to be alive and active in my mind again."

We returned to the city in the autumn, and that was the year that Hugh and I were together for two weeks out of the fifty-two. In the early autumn he went to Boston to play the lead roles in the newly formed Boston Repertory Company. Once it was established, the plan was for me to join him with our little one, and I would play some minor roles, a lovely thought—I missed being in the theatre. But the company was slow in establishing itself; perhaps the plays were too highbrow. Each Thursday evening the closing notice would be posted; each Saturday evening it would be taken down. There was no way I could go to Boston under those circumstances. I did go up for the opening of *The Road to Rome*, in which Hugh was superb as Hannibal—but even glowing notices were not enough to keep the company going, and in mid-winter they gave up and Hugh came home to a wife and daughter delighted to see him—though Hugh, like all actors I have known, was convinced when any show closed that he would never again get another job. However, the second day he was home he read for Alfred Lunt and Lynn Fontanne, who were producing Sam Behrman's *I Know My Love*. Hugh was signed for it, and exactly two weeks after his return from Boston he set off for a long pre-Broadway tour with the Lunts. I was a seasoned theatre wife. I rejoiced that he would be working with these great players, that we would have an assured income. But my acceptance of the way life works in the theatre did not stop loneliness. And Hugh missed me too. We began to think of alternate ways of life, of living full-time at Crosswicks.

The summer of Jo's fourth birthday we moved up to Crosswicks, having decided that we would take no more precautions, that if I got pregnant we would not move back to New York in the winter but would find some way of earning a living in the country.

Hugh had several summer-stock jobs, and of course I was working on a new novel. We were excited and little nervous about this very major decision. Within two months I was pregnant, and we were all set to become year-round country people.

One evening toward the end of the summer, when my pregnancy was well established, as was our decision to leave the city and the precarious world of the theatre and raise our children in the country, we were asked out for dinner in neighboring Cornwall. Among the guests was a well-known artist who had a summer place in that charming village. When he learned of our decision he warned us, urgently, that it is not good for the artist of any discipline to live in isolation, away from other artists. He told us that we would love being in the country the first year, that everything would be new and exciting, the beauty of autumn, the first snowstorm. But the artist needs to be in a city where there is the stimulation not only of other artists but of all kinds of people with brilliant and inquiring minds, to be surrounded by the stimulation of the city.

I listened. I listened well enough so that all these years later I remember the conversation almost verbatim. But I didn't, that evening, believe it. I was pregnant. I had my typewriter and records of classical music, books by great writers. Hugh and I had everything we needed. But the artist with his warning was right. The first year everything was strange and wonderful to this city girl. But ultimately Hugh and I were to experience the truth of his words.

Just as the summer season of stock was over, Hugh was asked to go with Judith Anderson to Berlin to play Aegeus, prince of Athens, in Robinson Jeffers's *Medea*.

Hugh had played Aegeus on Broadway and I had been tremendously proud of him: "Hugh is with Judith Anderson and John Gielgud in *Medea* and very happy about it. Yesterday when they had run through the first scene, Gielgud said, 'That was splendid, Aegeus, *splendid* for the first time without a book.' And when the rehearsal was over he said to him, 'We're very fortunate to have you with us.' "

And later: "The opening of *Medea* was very exciting. Hugh looked handsome beyond belief. Noël Coward sat exactly in front of me. During Hugh's scene he said, 'That man's good,' and when it was over he said, 'That guy gave an excellent performance.' And Judith Anderson told Toby, 'I think Hugh Franklin is the best man in the play—and I include John Gielgud.' And Coward wasn't heard to utter another word besides what he said about Hugh." Not only was playing Aegeus in Germany an opportunity Hugh shouldn't miss; Judith wanted him.

I was in Crosswicks while he was gone, and I remember sitting in the old white rocking chair we had found in the attic, holding Josephine and rocking and singing "Sweet and Low," with its "Bring him again to me."

It was a wonderful experience for Hugh, but then he came home to a pregnant wife, a beggaring house, a cold winter, and no job. He applied to the various factories in nearby Torrington, but he was rejected as a white-collar worker because he didn't have a degree in engineering, and as a blue-collar worker because he came out as "genius" on the tests. For a while he had a job as a shipping clerk in a small company, but it was hard on his back and John, our doctor and friend, said, "Hugh, you are not cut out for this kind of work."

It was a good thing he was unemployed when Bion was born because I had an even rougher time with him than I had had with Josephine, and I needed Hugh with me when I came home from the hospital.

But it was a different birthing. Instead of the impersonal treatment I had received in New York, this time I was surrounded with care. Hugh was with me, and so was one of our friends who was a nurse and who went to the hospital (the same hospital Hugh is in this summer) to special me. And our doctor was our friend.

I was very slow in dilating, but suddenly I said to our nurse friend, "I'm pushing."

"You can't be. You're only two fingers dilated."

"I'm pushing!"

She looked, shouted, "The baby's crowned!"

And Hugh saw the head of his son emerging from his wife.

It was, for me, a beautiful birth, and it was a glorious moment when John dropped my son between my breasts.

John was aware that the placenta might give trouble, and it did. I began to hemorrhage. The placenta wouldn't come and the bleeding wouldn't stop. Hugh was waiting in my room, but was sent downstairs when the babies were brought out for nursing. "Stick around, Hugh," John said, and poor Hugh spent a terrible time not knowing what was going on, but seeing doctors come running in, push the elevator button, and go up to the delivery-room floor. Finally I was brought down to the room and blood transfusions started. Hugh was called back and there was just time, once again, for us to kiss, to say "I love you," as I was wheeled off to the operating room.

When I got home from the hospital, our friends outdid themselves in bringing in food, helping with the baby. I nursed him, although I had lost so much blood that my milk was slow in coming, and for the first few weeks it had to be supplemented. He was given a bottle at night, and Hugh took on that feeding, holding and rocking his son, so that I could sleep and regain strength. But I nursed my baby, and this intimacy had an added poignancy because I knew that I could not have another baby.

By the time I was back on my feet Hugh had a job at the local radio station, but if he was going to make a career of radio it should be in New York, not northwest Connecticut.

We loved our house. We wanted a simple life for our children, with two full-time parents. In the center of the village was a nearly defunct general store which had been there for two centuries, flourishing in the early days of the village, gradually running down as the combustion engine came in and people could go farther afield to buy their harnesses, yard goods, groceries. The store had originally been owned by the family who now had one of the local banks. They didn't want it to go under completely, so they suggested to Hugh that he take it over, and they would finance it.

If that was a crazy suggestion for them to make to an actor with no experience whatsoever in business, it was crazy of Hugh to accept it. But I don't think I would love a man who never dared do anything crazy. When he went back to the theatre after nine years, that was crazy, too.

We learned a lot of hard lessons during our years at Crosswicks, years of raising our children, PTA, choir. One day I wrote in my journal, spotting it with tears: "We have come very sadly to the end of a regime. Poor little Touché had a heart attack and died. About one o'clock in the morning she woke me up, panting terribly. It was stifling hot, so I gave her some water, which she drank eagerly. And she just kept getting weaker and weaker. She's been part of my life for so long. I shall miss her in so many ways, at so many times. Even that last night when she was so sick she crawled into the baby's room and lay on the rug beside me when I nursed him."

We had kittens, got another dog. Animals have always been part of our lives. But Touché was special.

We learned a lot during our years on the store. I lost a good many illusions. I had thought that all that was needed for a perfect society was equal educational opportunities. In our village everybody went to the same school; I quickly learned that equal opportunity wasn't the be-all and end-all. I had thought that all farmers lived close to the land and God and were pure and noble. I learned that farmers are, by and large, just like the rest of us.

I overcame my residual shyness; one cannot be shy behind the counter. And there is much to be learned "on the other side of the counter" that cannot be learned in any other way. I learned about snobbery, and that people who were snobs were also people with no real "quality," as my mother would use that word. I learned a lot about human nature, and at times felt that we were running a free psychiatric clinic.

We worked very hard. But it was our store and it was honest sweat. Hugh got the idea of running off a weekly newspaper on the church mimeograph machine, with news of the village, birthdays, anniversaries, the week's specials. We were constantly covered with purple ink, but the newsletters worked, and business built up.

We made friends, lifelong friends who have supported us through the years, and through the storm of this summer.

Seven

*S*tormy indeed. When I kiss Hugh good night at bedtime, I do not know what the next day is going to bring. I remember being on a long hike where for the last few miles uphill it was only sheer willpower that kept my legs moving, one foot in front of the other, one foot in front of the other. This summer is like that. The prognosis is still optimistic, but there is a numbness deep in my heart. The fear that preceded the China trip is still with me.

Hugh does the best he can, tries to walk, to eat, to swim. One day he hands me *The New York Times* and says, "Here. I want you to read this."

"This" is a distressing article about parents in Tennessee who want to ban textbooks because they might "stimulate" the children's imaginations, and because in history books the chapter on the Renaissance "affirms the worth and dignity of man."

The article has come to Hugh's attention because similar parents are attacking my work as un-Christian. This startles me each time it happens, and it hurts. Or used to. Right now my attention is so focused on Hugh that there is no space in it for these attackers, who seem, at best, mildly insane. But it is typical of Hugh that he has noticed the article because of me, and his concern is a return to normal. Perhaps it will even increase his appetite, make him walk a little farther. Anything that holds his interest is improvement, and I am deeply moved that it has been awakened because of something which touches me. Hugh says of the attackers, "They are afraid," and I suspect that he is right.

How could I live, endure this summer, without imagination? How can anyone even begin to have an incarnational view of the universe without an incredible leap of the imagination? That God cares for us, every single one of us, so deeply that all power is willing to come to us, to be with us, takes all the imagination with which we have been endowed. And how could I get through this summer without affirming the worth and dignity of human beings? Isn't that what the incarnation was about? It is the message for me during these long weeks of Hugh's illness. During the interminable month of June when he was in the hospital I watched the doctors and nurses struggling with all their skill to affirm the dignity and worth of the patients. On the cancer floor this is no easy task. Hugh told of one of the nurses holding his head and the basin all through the night, while he retched and retched.

But to certain Christians it is un-Christian to affirm the dignity and worth of human beings. If that is so, then I cannot be a Christian. My husband, struggling to eat, to walk, to regain strength, sharing with me an article in the *Times* that caught his interest because of his concern for me, is an example of the dignity and worth of the human being in the place of excrement.

&. With my imagination I try to be hopeful, not unrealistically, but still hopeful that Hugh will get through this enough so that we will have more time together. But ultimately one of us will die before the other, unless we are killed together in an accident on one of our trips—not impossible in this age of terrorism. But if Hugh dies first, would I ever be able to stop saying "we" and say "I"? I doubt it. I do not think that death can take away the fact that Hugh and I are "we" and "us," a new creature born at the time of our marriage vows, which has grown along with us as our marriage has grown. Even during the times, inevitable in all marriages, when I have felt angry, or alienated, the instinctive "we" remains. And most growth has come during times of trial. Trial by fire. Fire as an image of purification is found all through literature. Dante speaks of the fire of roses. George MacDonald's Curdie has to plunge his hands deep into the burning fire of roses. In Scripture we read, "Our God is a consuming fire." God is "like a refiner's fire." Moses saw God in a burning bush, a bush which was burned and was not consumed, as we are to be burned by this holy fire and yet not consumed. We are to be refined in the fire like silver. Shadrach, Meshach, and Abednego walked through the flames. The Spirit descended and descends in tongues of fire.

Satan has tried to take fire over as his image, teasing, tormenting us with the idea of the flames of hell. Dante understood the wrongness of this in having the most terrible circle of hell be *cold*.

Coldness of the last circle of hell; coldness of heart; lack of compassion; treating people as objects (a reasonable definition of pornography, Hugh says); pride; setting ourselves apart from the "others"—all these are cold.

It is a terrible choice: the purifying fire of the Creator or the deathly cold fire of Satan.

It is the fire this summer, and I can only pray that it will be purifying.

* * *

‍‍‍❧ I spend a week going back and forth to Wesleyan University in Middletown, Connecticut, a little over an hour from Crosswicks. When I accepted the job of teaching one of the workshops at this excellent writers' conference I had expected to be there for the full five days, but with Hugh's illness this is impossible. I feel that I must honor my commitment, however, and kind friends are arranging daily transportation so that I can commute.

Even the day I leave, there is yet another setback, a massive increase in what was a slight diabetic neuropathy in Hugh's feet and lower legs, but which now makes him walk tentatively, like an old man—another side effect of the platinum chemotherapy.

My workshop is full of talented writers, but it is physically a rough week, with the commuting back and forth. As well as teaching my daily workshop, I have to give half-hour conferences to twenty-five people, which I couldn't possibly have managed on my own. With the help of my friend Jane, they are scheduled, fitted in catch-as-catch-can.

During one conference someone said, "We've been talking about your amazing optimism."

The men and women in my workshop had been told the reason for my commuting, why I could not be at the conference full-time, but this student was referring not so much to Hugh's illness as to a general attitude toward life.

And I heard myself saying, "I do not believe that true optimism can come about except through tragedy." Sometimes so casually is revelation given.

It has been a rough year (I still think of the year in terms of the academic year), starting in January with the death of publisher and friend Harold Shaw. It was not an unexpected death.

He had been struggling valiantly with cancer for eighteen months. But it was grievous, and death when it finally comes is always unexpected. It came at what was for Hugh and me a time of joy. As our fortieth anniversary approached, our children began talking about a party for us. One evening I said to Hugh, "I know you don't want a party. Why don't you take me someplace warm for a few days?"

So he arranged a trip on a small ship puttering about the Virgin Islands. We didn't escape the party entirely; our dozen or so godchildren in New York had a surprise dinner party for us the night before we left. Not totally "surprise." I was asked to make the salad.

The next day, the twenty-sixth, the day of the anniversary, we flew to St. Thomas and boarded our little ship. The other passengers were pleasant, the food excellent, and what I liked best of all was that almost every day the ship would drop anchor, the swimming platform would be put out, and we could drop off it right into the ocean.

One morning I was sitting out on deck writing in my journal and I was suddenly assailed by a wave of passionate grief. Hugh came out and looked at me, asking, "What's the matter?"

"I don't know."

"You look as though you're about to burst into tears."

"I know."

"What is it?"

"I don't know."

When we got home we learned that this wave of grief had come about at the time of Harold's death.

Not long after that, there was the shocking and unexpected and ambiguous death of one of our godsons at the age of twenty-nine. He had lived with us for nearly a year, during which time we had given him his twenty-first birthday party. Hugh bought him a brown corduroy suit, of which he was enormously proud. We had talked deeply with this young artist about the dark side of human nature, our own shadow selves, as real and important to us as the more visible self. We talked of the *terror anticus* which besets the human being, particularly one who has chosen to work in theatre, music, literature. We told him that the word *panic* comes from the ancient Pan, who, when the *terror anticus* came upon him, would pull out his pipes and try to play himself back into peace.

We had seen our godson only a few days before his death, laughing, radiant, having done a good job and knowing he had done it well. So why did he, like Orson, go out a window to his death? I thought of Orson swimming back to Sconset, desperately fighting the tide as the urge for life overtook the urge for death. And then doing the irrevocable. Did our godson, at the moment of descent, want to stop the fall, to return to life? Too late, too late. This death was irrational and inexplicable and unnecessary, and we were angry as well as grieved.

Another friend called after a double mastectomy. One thing after another, one thing after another, as so often happens. And now Hugh's cancer. But when I told Carol, earlier in the summer, that I was keeping my faith, part of what I meant was that my attitude toward the universe, and the ultimate working out of pattern and purpose, had not changed. Terrible things happen, and God does not prevent them. But the purpose of a universe created by a loving Maker is to be trusted.

❧ The student who remarked on my optimism and I talk a little further about my belief that God is not going to fail with Creation, no matter how abominably we human beings abuse free will, no matter how we keep our own self-interest in mind rather than the working out of a Grand Unified Theory. We talk about how God can come into "the flame of incandescent terror" and purify even the most terrible anguish.

It is not an easy conversation for me under the circumstances, but I learn from it.

Teaching a course in techniques of fiction involves sharing, no matter how indirectly, one's attitude toward the human endeavor. Maritain wrote that "fiction differs from every other art in one respect: it concerns the conduct of life itself." Thus any discussion of the writing of fiction is theological, even if God is never mentioned.

It is good for me to teach because it draws me out of myself and the limiting aspects of Hugh's illness. Severe illness isolates those in close contact with it, because it inevitably narrows the focus of concern. To a certain extent this can lead to healing, but not if the circle of concern is so tight that it cannot be broken into, or out of. Our circle widens with each phone call, each visitor. The workshop at Wesleyan helps me focus on the true concerns of the human endeavor. It does not lessen my love for my husband, or the deep interior prayer which goes on all the time. Rather it strengthens it, as I am forced to articulate ideas and hopes which are often latent.

I get home one afternoon and go out into the garden to pick lettuce, and hear a small sound and turn. There, caught in the net trellis which holds up the snap peas, is a small bird, a female finch. She stays very still, one wing outspread. I have brought a kitchen knife with me, and cut away the twine of the trellis until she is able to fly away, soaring, free.

Where is someone to cut us out of the net?

One thing goes wrong for Hugh after another. He still cannot swallow anything solid. Finally the gastroenterologist takes him as an outpatient to the operating room in the hospital to look down his esophagus and into his stomach and cannot look, because there is a stricture in the esophagus, almost closing it completely just at the entrance to the stomach. No wonder Hugh has not been able to eat! The doctor opens the esophagus, a very painful procedure. The peptic ulcers are healing, but the fungus is still on the esophagus and has caused the scarring which has almost closed it.

The cure seems worse than the disease.

If I feel caught in the net like that little bird, what must it be like for Hugh, with his body betraying him over and over again?

Hugh is an actor. For the actor, as for the dancer, the body is the instrument. I can walk away from the typewriter or the piano; although they seem to be part of me, in actuality they are not. But Hugh's instrument is his body, his beautiful body. He has always been tall and lean. He has felt legitimate pride in his body, and has kept it well.

When the urologist first talked to us about the procedure for Hugh's kind of cancer, and explained that it included the removal of the bladder, and the consequent use of a bag, I talked to him about this, saying that anything that changes the body is more painful and humiliating to an actor or dancer than it would be for the rest of us. I don't know whether or not he understood. He is a doctor, interested in curing disease. But curing disease is inextricably intertwined with the psyche. We are not body alone.

I wish I could take the kitchen knife and cut away the cords that are binding Hugh and free him.

My friend Dana and I talk about how we want to make everything all right for those we love, and cannot. Her mother died of pancreatic cancer only a few months ago. We say to each other that if we were God we would make everything all right, and then we stop. Look at each other. Because we suddenly see that making everything all right would *not* make everything all right. We would not be human beings. We would then be no more than puppets obeying the strings of the master puppeteer. We agree sadly that it is a good thing that we are not God; we do not have to understand God's ways, or the suffering and brokenness and pain that sooner or later come to us all.

But we do have to know in the very depths of our being that the ultimate end of the story, no matter how many aeons it takes, is going to be all right.

&. We try to keep things as normal for Hugh as possible, have friends in for dinner. One of Laurie's colleagues, a cardiac specialist, comes on a gentle summer evening with his wife and young son. The family has been friends of Hugh's through watching him as Dr. Tyler on ABC's *All My Children*. The night Hugh had to return to the hospital with his heart galloping arrhythmically, and this gentle doctor was brought in, he greeted Hugh with affection, "Why, Dr. Tyler!"

Our tree-planting godchildren come again and of course more trees must be planted. One of our summer projects has been expanding our little terrace so that it is more functional, and Hugh has been able to watch the progress from the kitchen windows. We buy seven small hemlocks to make a tiny border, and Hugh calls instructions through the windows as we dig and plant, naming each little tree for one of the seven seas. I mostly stand and encourage while the young people do the hard work. When they come in, grubby and tired, Hugh says, "You've done a fine job. Now just move them all three inches to the right."

Laughter heals, heals those who ache for what Hugh is enduring.

Another evening Scott and Lily Peck and their son, Christopher, come for dinner. It is a beautiful evening and both before and after dinner we relax out on the expanded terrace, and Hugh is suddenly and beautifully fully there, his most real self. We are all aware that it is a special evening. Later Scotty wrote to me: ". . . but that evening in early August was quite extraordinary, as you yourself recognized. Fortunately or unfortunately, I am not one of those people given to seeing auras or whatnot. But Hugh just glowed. He glowed all over. It was one of the most extraordinary phenomenons which I have ever been privileged to witness. There were two things about it. One was the light. His whole being, despite being physically wasted, seemed to have become a being of light. The other was his absolutely extraordinary alertness. Despite his illness and disease, despite his age, despite his deafness, I have never seen any human being for a period of several hours so alert. It manifested itself in a hundred different ways. He spontaneously asked about the Foundation and how it was doing. I wouldn't even have believed that he would have remembered. He not only allowed Christopher and me to go out into the garden to have a smoke, but even wondered for us whether it wasn't time for us to do so. Et cetera, et cetera. I could go on and on, but I have never been in the presence of any human being who was, in fact, so present."

᛭ Being present is part of the actor's training. It is also Hugh's special gift. The most terrible time in our marriage came when, for one reason or other, he was not present for me.

The near-decade we lived year-round in Crosswicks was a rough one. A lonely decade. We were constantly exhausted, as young working parents often are. Bringing a dead store back to life was a draining job. Hugh often came home so tired that he was anything but present.

Four of our closest friends died within two years of each other, and that is a lot of bereavement for a couple in their thirties to go through. On the eighth of January 1955, I wrote: "Arthur Farmer is dead. This is something I haven't realized yet. I was, as usual, to have dinner with him when I went to New York." Such New York trips were rare, usually to see editor or agent. I often stayed with Liz, who had stood up with me at our wedding, and her husband, also Arthur. They often visited us at Crosswicks and we were warm, deep friends. The two Arthurs were very different in temperament and looks, but two men we trusted implicitly.

That January afternoon I checked in with Liz and Arthur, told them I wouldn't be late, and went to meet Arthur Farmer. He was about to leave for a vacation with the John Steinbecks, but as soon as I got to his apartment it was obvious that he was ill and in pain. He insisted on going out to a nearby restaurant, but he couldn't eat, and I took him home and called his doctor, and it was decided that I should take him to the hospital in a taxi. Even though he was weak and in pain his voice was perfectly strong and steady and his pulse, which I had taken several times during the evening, was, though a little rapid, not terribly so. I don't think it occurred to Arthur that he was dying, and it didn't to me.

In the morning when I called the hospital, he was dead. His doctor had wanted to reach me, but had no idea where I was staying.

I had a husband and little ones to go home to, and Hugh could share in my grief. But we seemed inundated by death. A year later the other Arthur, Liz's husband, was dead of a heart attack, and eleven months later Liz was dead of a cerebral hemorrhage. That was how our daughter Maria came to us, a legacy from Liz and Arthur, a seven-year-old little girl, suddenly and unexpectedly orphaned. Don, my breakfast companion and mentor, was found dead in his garden. We seemed surrounded by death, the death of those close to us, the death of neighbors. In a small village it is evident that no man is an island. The white-pillared church was across from our store, and when there was a death the bell tolled.

Financially we were close to the edge. We could not afford to heat the water for daily baths for everybody, so twice a week I filled the tub with hot water and put the children in with me. Eventually the store did well enough so that we could afford private baths.

How we managed as well as we did I'm not sure. We were certainly naïve in all country ways. One day a farmer came into the store and asked Hugh if he had a church key. The church was right across the street from the store, so Hugh said he didn't have one, but he'd go see if he could get one. That was how he learned that "church key" was a name for a can opener in those days when soda and beer cans didn't have automatic tabs. Less amusing was bringing home the wilted produce, the dented cans.

I spent three hours or more a day in the store. I was struggling to write, to keep house, help in the store, be a good mother, and yet improve my skills as a storyteller. And that decade was one of rejection slips. I would mutter as I cleaned house, "Emily Brontë didn't have to run the vacuum cleaner. Jane Austen didn't do the cooking." Often when Hugh came home from the store in the evening he was too exhausted to be affectionate, or to understand how wounded I was from all the rejection slips for work I believed in. Failure itself is exhausting.

I loved my children, but I hungered for adult conversation. One day after a rare evening alone I wrote: "I keep thinking about the evening we had together last night, my darling husband, alone by candlelight and firelight, and the way we were able to talk. We are practically never alone together and this is a bad thing. No matter how much we love our children there are many things we cannot talk about in front of them, things that we need from time to time to say. Let us try to remember for their sakes as well as ours that every once in a while for our development we must be alone."

As soon as Bion, our baby, was in nursery school, I dropped out of the group of mothers who occasionally gathered together to drink coffee and gossip. This was writing time. Nobody else needed writing time. And I felt that I was looked at askance because I spent so much time at the typewriter and yet couldn't sell what I wrote. I certainly wasn't pulling my weight financially.

In my journal I wrote: "There is a gap in understanding between me and our friends and acquaintances. I can't quite understand a life without books and study and music and pictures and a driving passion. And they, on the other hand, can't understand why I *have* to write, *why* I am a writer. When, for instance, I say to someone that I have to get home to work, the assumption is that I mean housecleaning or ironing, not writing a book. I'm very kindly permitted to be a writer but not to take time in pursuing my trade. Nor can they understand the importance of music, or why an hour with a Mozart sonata at the piano is *not* wasted time but time spent on a real value. Or really listening, without talking, to music. Or going for a walk simply to see the beauty around one, or the real importance of a view from a window."

The people I felt easiest with during my hours in the store were the carnival men who wintered at the nearby fairgrounds, going over the merry-go-rounds and Ferris wheels, maintaining the equipment. They said what they felt, even if it included rough language. But I had already heard all the rough language from the stagehands. It didn't shock me. Often I had to translate what our regular customers said into what they actually meant. The carnival men were far more direct. In early November I asked them how they were going to cook Thanksgiving dinner. They laughed and said they'd open some cans of hash or beans to cook over their Sterno. So I roasted their Thanksgiving turkey for them.

One of Hugh's favorite stories is of the day when two of the carnival men were in the store just before noon. One of them asked him, "Where's the boss?"

"What do you mean?" he demanded. "I'm the boss."

"Oh, come on, we know who the boss is."

Hugh was behind the meat counter slicing cold cuts and at that moment I walked in. "Madeleine!" he called. "Down on your knees!"

Of course I immediately dropped to my knees.

The carnival men thought that this was wonderful, and after that they treated me like a princess. On Wednesdays, my day to close the store in the evening, a couple of them would wander in just before closing time, to buy a packet of gum or a candy bar, and wait while I closed the cash register, put the day's take in a canvas bag and then in my pocket. They would wait while I closed and locked the building; wait till I had the car started, not always easy in winter. Nothing was ever said, but I felt completely protected by their concern.

I was fine with the carnival men, but in other ways I felt as inadequate socially as I had in Jacksonville. And how could I call myself a writer? I had a few poems published in very small magazines. I sold two stories during that decade, one to *Fantastic Universe*, one to *Gent*, and one novel, *A Winter's Love*, which was published (after a number of rejections) by Lippincott and disappeared with hardly a trace.

I was homesick for New York. I wanted to be challenged and stimulated by people who were brighter than I. I felt that Hugh was wasting his talent in the store, although I admired the way he built it up into a viable business.

If sometimes he was too worn out to be affectionate he showed his love powerfully by taking the children to school with him in the morning on his way to the store—he had had breakfast with them first, thus giving me the chance to write at night, and sleep an hour or so later in the morning.

In the evening when he got home from the store, we had Quiet Hour. Anybody was invited who wanted to sit and have serious conversation; mostly the kids chose to do something else. As I heard Hugh's car door slam, I would put a match to the kindling and light the fire (as I look back on those years, it was always winter). At dinner we were the whole family, together, but until the children were older and we were back in New York we had that one hour before dinner to ourselves.

And there were some wonderful moments, some beautiful memories. One winter when Bion was a baby there was a three-day ice storm, and although we kept fires going in the two fireplaces the house got colder and colder. On the third day, friends who heated by kerosene or coal and were not dependent on an oil furnace took the children. Hugh and I cooked dinner over the coals, then built up the fire and lay on the floor, looking into the flames and talking deeply in our amazing solitude.

And then we made love.

Eight

---

*O*h, my love.

When we first learned of Hugh's cancer I was dry as the parched land suffering drought in the Southeast. Now the tears are close to the surface. For the third time this summer I come to the Psalms for the evening of the fourth day and read, "My God, my God, why have you forsaken me?" and the tears rush out silently and stream down my face. Music, too, tends to pluck at the chords of emotion. Tears are healing. I do not want to cry when I am not alone, but by myself I don't try to hold the tears back. In a sense this solitary weeping is a form of prayer.

But things continue to go wrong. Hugh gets a bladder infection. What next?

One morning he starts uncontrollable vomiting. It goes on and on. He cannot even take the antibiotic for the urinary-tract infection, though it is in liquid form. He returns to the hospital, through the emergency room, hoping to be treated only as an outpatient until the vomiting is controlled. But despite his reluctance, it is evident that he must be admitted. The doctors are baffled and discouraged. Hugh's appetite should have returned weeks ago; he should have been gaining strength. He should have had the surgery and be recuperating by now.

John, our old friend and general practitioner, had sent a patient of his to visit Hugh when he was first in the hospital, a man in his fifties who had had the same surgery Hugh is facing, who now drives a school bus, goes fishing, considers himself, three years after surgery, to be cured. What is happening with Hugh? Where will all this end? Can I believe that he, too, will be cured? What about all those prayers with which he is surrounded? I know that these prayers are faithfully coming. I believe in them. What is happening?

The days drag on. I am overimpatient that the doctors cannot find out why Hugh cannot eat solid food. I expect too much of ordinary human beings who happen to have more training in medicine than the rest of us. They are not gods. They are doing their best. I must watch out for false expectations.

And I must have realistic but not false expectations of myself. It is all a delicate and difficult balance. Sometimes I am strong with that wonderful strength which is not my own but is given (much of it through the prayers which steadfastly keep coming); and sometimes I crumple. At four o'clock this morning I sat up in bed and wept, sitting up to weep because to cry lying down makes one's nose stuffy. And to let go, at four o'clock in the morning, is all right.

I have been looking over my old journals (something I seldom do) as I relive the volatile years of our marriage. It has been fun to relive our early years in the theatre, our courtship, stormy though it was, the birth of our babies. Sometimes I come upon unexpected things. In one entry, written during our early years at Crosswicks, I read: "They said in college that there was one housemother who was a widow and who could not go to sleep without a green velvet arm in bed with her." I think of being in bed alone and wonder if I will ever wake in the night and not stretch out foot or hand to touch the living flesh of my beloved. I ache for that strange housemother, although I know that, whatever happens, I will never want a green velvet arm. I have left behind forever the "blankie" and the favorite stuffed animal.

So I sleep alone. In the morning I swim for half an hour before breakfast, do whatever needs to be done, make myself a sandwich and a thermos of soup, and spend the rest of the day in the hospital.

One morning during my pre-breakfast swim, I remember some words Helen Waddell wrote about prayer, and go to look them up in my big brown Goody Book where I have copied them down: "They asked the abbot Macarius, saying, 'How ought we to pray?' and the old man said, 'There is no need of much speaking in prayer, but often stretch out thy hands and say, 'Lord, as Thou wilt and as Thou knowest, have mercy upon me.' But if there is war in thy soul, add, 'Help me,' and because he knoweth what we have need of he sheweth us his mercy."

Help, I cry. *Help!*

In the mail I get a loving note from Mother Ruth of the community of the Holy Spirit. She enclosed a little card from England printed with the words: "He setteth in pain the jewels of his love." They are good words. They could equally be reversed: God can provide the setting in which the pearl of pain is placed.

We learn to live in the cloud of unknowing, not only the cloud of God's mystery, but the cloud of unknowing what is going to happen from day to day. That is always true, but when things go along routinely we are less aware of it. Something unexpected seems to happen every day this summer. One problem for Hugh is cleared up, and immediately something else occurs. The doctors, who were calmly optimistic in May, are less certain as we move toward September.

In *The Irrational Season* I wrote that when two people truly love each other, each one must be willing to let the other die first. I may be reluctantly, painfully willing, but I could understand a clean death better than this nibbling away at the man I have loved for so many years.

I have a friend whose husband is being taken away from her by Alzheimer's disease, so that he is a senile wreck of what was once a handsome, virile, dominant man. That is far worse than this. There are many people in situations far more terrible than ours. But there is a quality of limbo to this unknowing.

• Hugh has his seventieth birthday in the hospital. He has reached the Biblical age, three score years and ten. "And if by reason of strength they be fourscore years, yet is their strength labour and sorrow, for it is soon cut off and we fly away." Labour and sorrow and it is over too soon. I come from a long-lived family. So does Hugh. Seventy does not seem old.

Earlier in the summer I had talked to our children about wanting a special surprise for Hugh for this birthday, perhaps a little trip together. When he became ill, but with a hopeful prognosis, we decided on a birthday dinner, and I hoped that it would be in celebration of his recovery, and we would invite his doctors It is all right, it is healthy to dream.

Back in June when Josephine was East for Léna's and Charlotte's graduations, and Hugh was in the hospital, she bought her ticket from San Francisco so that she could be here for the birthday dinner. Now she is coming, simply to be with us, to see her father. Maria, our younger daughter, with a brand-new baby at home (our joy, this difficult summer), and another baby only a year and a half old, will be able to be present only by phone.

Léna and Charlotte, living together in our apartment in New York, come up by bus, arriving the day before their mother. That evening, according to tradition, we make hot cocoa and climb up into the high four-poster bed with volumes of Shakespeare. We have read, during several summers, various comedies, taking turns with the roles. I refuse to read *Hamlet* because, of course, we all want to play Hamlet.

We read together, a scene or two, but our minds are not on Shakespeare or his characters, this night, two nights before their grandfather's seventieth birthday. It is their first encounter with the life-threatening illness of someone they love. We talk, about their summer jobs, about college coming up in a month, about family, about love. Simply being together is good.

We will not be able to have the celebratory party we had hoped for. Nothing has gone as expected. Despite my love for my grand-daughters, my pleasure at their presence, I feel that there is a black hole in the middle of my sternum.

Josephine comes, and we hold each other closely, physical touch saying what words, at this moment, cannot say. We call Maria, with whom I have been talking daily. A week earlier Bion and Laurie and I left Hugh well tended in the hospital and took the three-hour drive to see the new baby, an adorable little thing with soft strawberry-blond hair. Brought back a picture to show his grandfather. It is hard to be so far away, but good that the phone keeps us daily in touch.

At the hospital the nurses are enthusiastic about our coming with presents and ice cream for Hugh. We promise to keep the door closed and not disturb the other patients. Later in the evening the nurses themselves come in with a birthday cake, which they can eat and enjoy even if Hugh can't. His sense of humor despite his constant discomfort has made him loved.

Hugh and Charlotte have always celebrated their birthdays—which are only two days apart—together. When Charlotte was littler she was usually asked if she'd rather not have a "regular" birthday party with other children, and her immediate response was always, "No, I'd rather have my birthday with Gum." Gum. The children's name for their grandfather, a diminutive of Hugh's suggestion of "Grumpy Old Grampa"—Grumpy Old Gramdpa having been one of his more spectacularly successful roles in high school!

But this summer there can be no elegant evening party for Charlotte and Gum; a seventeen-year-old tradition is unwillingly being broken. We have, instead, that evening after we come home from the hospital, a triple party at Crosswicks, not only for Charlotte but for Léna and Josephine, whose June birthdays got lost in the shuffle of the girls' graduation festivities. We make an effort. Have presents for everybody. And I think of Hugh in the hospital with the deadly dull anti-reflux diet, unable to be with us tonight on this, his special day.

It has suddenly turned cold, this twenty-fourth day of August, and when I walk the dogs after dinner the stars are brilliant. The sight of a night sky with the great river of our galaxy streaming across the dark always fills me with hope. This night, what can I hope for?

I cry out, "Oh, God, resolve this!" The surgery cannot go on and on being postponed, but Hugh is not yet strong enough for such major trauma. The post-platinum problems surely should be letting up by now, but they are not. Doctors do not like to be unsuccessful, do not like to be unable to understand what is going on. Do not like, perhaps, to be reminded that they are only human beings with medical training and a certain amount of expertise acquired in their years of practice. I don't require that they be gods. All I care is that they continue to care.

Again I am grateful that Hugh is not in a big city hospital. The total loss of independence, of privacy, is devastating at best. Specimens are taken of blood, of urine, of stools. But here the nurses and technicians are compassionate and caring, as perhaps it is impossible to be in a huge city hospital with overcrowding of patients and even greater understaffing of nurses and aides. Two of the floor nurses talk with me of their own fathers going through much the same experience that Hugh is enduring. They joke with Hugh, laugh at his unique humor, which amazingly keeps breaking through.

The esophagus has to be opened again. The esophagitis is still acute. Surgery can't keep being postponed. Is he strong enough to go through the operation? Decisions will be made soon. He has an ultrasound scan; there is to be another cystoscopy.

But I am grateful beyond words for the community which surrounds me. I am not alone, as so many people in today's society are alone. The family is staunchly with me. Here on this floor of the hospital I now know most of the nurses by name. When fruit juice or ginger ale is brought around for the patients, I am included. Charlie, the interim minister from our Congregational Church, comes faithfully to call, to sit and talk, a real visit. There are cards and flowers from various members of the church, although Hugh and I are there only in the summer, unable to be the active members we used to be when we lived at Crosswicks year round. Prayers for Hugh and me continue to uphold and strengthen, and are an affirmation that what is going on in our lives matters. There is a feeling of being an interdependent part of the whole human predicament, a oneness with other patients, other anxious families, a oneness even with people's tragedies as we read about them in the paper.

This oneness is consistent with what we now know of the nature of creation as understood in terms of particle physics. We seem to have forgotten this oneness, this interdependence, with our different countries, languages, religions, factions within religions, with our nuclear families frequently isolated from grandparents, aunts, uncles. We desperately need to remember that we are each part of one another.

John Gribbin in his book *In Search of Schrödinger's Cat* writes: "Particles that were once together in an interaction remain in some sense part of a single system, which responds together to future reactions. Virtually everything we see and touch and feel is made up of collections of particles that have been involved in interactions with other particles right back through time, to the Big Bang in which the universe as we know it came into being. The atoms in my body are made of particles that once jostled in close proximity in the cosmic fireball with particles that form the body of some living creature on some distant, undiscovered planet. Indeed, the particles that make up my body once jostled in close proximity and interacted with the particles that make up your body. We are . . . parts of a single system."

In the act of making love two separate people come together to make one, in a struggle to return to that original unity. In this action of love we are truly part of one another and this unity carries over into our daily living. Is this why the thought of separation by death is so excruciatingly painful? One time when I had returned home after a speaking engagement I said to Hugh, as we sat in the kitchen talking while I cooked dinner, "Wherever I go, you are with me." Won't this always be true?

If we human beings were truly aware that all creation is a

unity, as two lovers are aware of unity, wouldn't we treat each other better? There have been many signs of a newly awakened caring in recent years, and I need to remember all the signs of goodness and hope, particularly after I look at the paper or listen to the news. We are one planet, a single organism. What happens on this floor makes a difference everywhere.

For the entire universe with its countless galaxies is the setting for this pearl of pain.

&. My theological reading for the past several years has been in the area of astrophysics, particle physics, quantum mechanics. These disciplines are dealing with the nature of being, and I find that much theology founders over peripheral things, gets stuck on a limited literalism. But the amazing discoveries in the world of physics reveal a universe which is enormous beyond comprehension.

Who is this creator to whom I cry out, "Help!" How can I believe in a God who cares about individual lives on one small and unimportant planet? I don't know. I just don't know. But I cannot turn away from the hope and the mystery which can never be understood. I know only that when I cry out, "Help!" the fact that I am crying out affirms that somewhere in some part of me I hope that there is someone who hears, who cares. The One I cry out to is not limited by size or number, and can be glimpsed only in metaphor, that chief tool of imagery of the poet. And it is only in the high language of poetry that anything can be said about God. Hildegard of Bingen likened herself to "a feather on the breath of God." Lady Julian of Norwich saw the entire universe in a hazelnut.

This summer I find reality in the simple things of creation.

We have enjoyed food with a special poignancy. After a long day sitting with Hugh in the hospital, seeing time go by, and no improvement, I am exhausted when I get home, more psychically than physically. Most nights Bion cooks out on the Weber. A chicken stuffed with lemons that send their moisture throughout the flesh is delicious, served with vegetables from the garden, and a big salad. If it is at all possible we sit out on the terrace to eat, and watch the sunset; the clouds are achingly beautiful. Now at the end of August the night is coming earlier, and we stay to watch the first stars. I am deeply, piercingly rejoicing in the beauty of this gentle New England countryside. Across the fields are the woods and then the ancient hills—from whence cometh my help.

What happens when we give up our matter at death? Do we still matter? As I sit here in Hugh's hospital room with my little typewriter on my lap, he is up in the OR having another cystoscopy. I look at a charming mobile of shells hanging from his IV pole, a birthday present. The thoughtfulness of this gift makes it especially precious.

Every morning before breakfast, while I swim, I silently recite various verses I have memorized. The movement of the body through water helps mind and heart to work together. When I have finished with my alphabet of memorized poems and prayers, I have swum for well over half an hour. It is a good way of timing my swimming, and by holding on to the great affirmations of the Psalms, of Coverdale and Cranmer, of John Donne and Henry Vaughan and Thomas Browne, I am sustained by the deep rhythm of their faith.

I need faith. Oh, I need it.

The news is bad. The tests have revealed that the cancer has spread outside the bladder and into the ureters. Radiation treatment is being started this afternoon. Was all the suffering caused by the platinum for nothing? Don't I truly believe that there is nothing which is for nothing?

I ask the urologist, "What's the prognosis?"

He says, "Well, it's a very aggressive cancer."

I say, "I don't want him nibbled to death. I've felt all summer that Hugh is being nibbled to death by sharks. I don't want that."

He says, "I know what you mean." He understands. And yet what can he do?

We shake hands. I say, "Thank you, Herb." Doctors do not like to fail. It is even harder on them because Laurie is their colleague.

And this is the night we're having a dozen or more people in for a cookout and a swim, the wonderful young people who have worked on house and terrace all summer. We've added a screened porch, with a bedroom above it for Bion and Laurie, who badly need their own space, and we want to thank these young men who are truly artisans in the old-fashioned sense of the word. They have made the addition look as though it's been part of the old house forever. It does not stick out as new, but belongs.

What a night to be having a party, when our hearts are heavy, when anxiety has risen again in my throat like gorge. But two of the boys are going back to college; this is Labor Day weekend and some schools have already started. We cannot put it off. For their sakes I have to be composed if not merry.

As for Hugh, he is good, so good. As our granddaughter Léna said at the time of his birthday, "He's a trouper." He is.

My God, my God, why have you forsaken me? In just a few days it will be time for that Psalm to come around for the fourth time since the verdict that the cancer was not the expected small and easily controlled one.

My God, my God, why? People have asked this in times of

anguish throughout the centuries, in times of plague, in times of war, in times of personal tragedy. It is all right to ask why.

Why? I ask, knowing that there are no easy answers, perhaps no answers at all.

My friend Tallis remarked once that cancer is the result of sin, not the sin of the person suffering from this ugly disease, but the sins of many human beings throughout the ages, making wrong choices, letting greed override wisdom.

This abuse of free will throughout the millennia does not mean that cancer is a punishment, as some people view it. No, it is a consequence of many actions by many people, often unknowing. Those first factories of the Industrial Revolution fouled the once clean sky, but it was not a conscious fouling. People did not understand what they were doing. When Hugh smoked as a young man, smoking was not yet seen as a threat to health. My grandfather smoked moderately all his life, and he lived to be a hundred and one, but our planet's air and water were far cleaner than they are now.

I have become phobic about smoking (I was one of the lucky people who never liked it), and I bitterly resent being made a "passive smoker." It is particularly bad in airports, but wherever people smoke, those of us who do not are made to suffer from the addiction and discourtesy of those who do. Even in this hospital, there is only one waiting room on all seven floors where smoking is prohibited—the meditation room on the cancer floor. When Hugh has come in as an outpatient for one procedure or another and I am told to wait in the lobby, I reply politely but firmly, "No." When I get a surprised look I say, "I will not wait where there are smokers. The smoke gets in my contact lenses and irritates my eyes. I will wait in the meditation room on the third floor. If it is occupied I will wait out in the corridor."

I am told that soon the hospital will be entirely smoke-free, and the only reason this eminently sensible decision has not already been implemented is that some of the older doctors will not give up their cigarettes.

Consequences: cancer is a result of consequences. It is not sent as a punishment. I do not have to make the repulsive theological error of feeling that I have to see cancer as God's will for my husband. I do not want anything to do with that kind of God. Cancer is not God's will. The death of a child is not God's will. The deaths from automobile accidents during this long holiday weekend are not God's will. I would rather have no God at all than that kind of punitive God. Tragedies are consequences of human actions, and the only God worth believing in does not cause the tragedies but lovingly comes into the anguish with us.

Alas, we human beings have played god throughout the centuries. We do not play god well. Look what we have done.

What is the difference between playing god and making responsible decisions? That is always a question the doctor must ask. And so must the rest of us. How do we separate self-interest from what is right for others? How do we love without manipulating or wanting to control? Do heads of state ever completely avoid that corruption which Lord Acton warns comes from power?

Right now the doctors have absolute power over Hugh. I have to trust them to ask the right questions. I have seen some doctors let the vanity of their profession make them prolong dying or, what is even worse, abandon their patient. I trust Hugh's doctors to listen to Hugh. To listen to me when I talk to them. I trust them to take into account that sometimes death is better than keeping a patient alive just to keep him alive. I trust them not to prolong the dying when it is time for death.

Of course they see death as failure. I have to trust them to be willing to fail.

 If we are not willing to fail we will never accomplish anything. All creative acts involve the risk of failure. Marriage is a terrible risk. So is having children. So is giving a performance in the theatre, or the writing of a book. Whenever something is completed successfully, then we must move on, and that is again to risk failure.

Hugh made a success of the store. We were making a reasonable living. But there was nowhere further to go with the store; it had reached a plateau. If we were not to remain stuck in the place we were in, we had to move on, somewhere, somehow.

One evening Hugh and I were amazingly alone, the three children all at someone else's house. This seldom happened, and we were enjoying sitting quietly in front of the fire. I turned to Hugh, asking, "Darling, are you still happy with the store?"

"No."

"Then sell it."

It was a major decision. It would totally disrupt our comfortable life. It would turn our security upside down.

In the autumn we used to take one night away and go farther north into New England to buy cheese, going on back roads to out-of-the-way farms. We returned to the store laden with cheeses, and their sale paid for our little jaunt.

That autumn of 1958 we had bought a dozen or so cheeses and were relaxing in a comfortable room in an inn. Hugh looked at me and quoted from Milton: "That one Talent which is death to hide."

"You have to go back to the theatre." I reached out for his

hand. Acting was his talent. It could not go on being pushed aside. He had proven to himself, to the world, that he could make a living outside the theatre. It was time to go back.

I was more than ready to return to New York, but the idea of the total disruption of their lives was frightening to our children.

If Hugh, this summer, is controlled by the decisions of the physicians, so our children were controlled by ours.

Amazingly, we were able to sell the store, and well. I gave up my jobs of directing the choir, of working with the young people. We knew that moving our children out of a small dairy-farm village and back to the city would be a shocking change for them, so we decided to bridge the two disparate lives by taking them on a real family vacation, a ten-week camping trip from the Atlantic to the Pacific and back again. We had a wonderful time, tent camping. I cooked our meals on the fire which Hugh had built. We had an unhurried opportunity to see the greatness and beauty of our native land. Hugh, negative about picnics ("Why eat outdoors with flies and bugs when we get just as good a view from the dining-room table?"), had suggested and enjoyed a ten-week picnic. (According to our children, he hasn't been on one since.)

Before leaving on our trip, we spent a night in New York, talking with old theatre friends. Hugh asked Thelma, the stage manager, "Do you think I'm crazy to think of coming back to the theatre?"

Thelma replied calmly, "Anybody is crazy to work in the theatre, but if it's your talent it's what you have to do."

Hugh also made contact with several agents and producers, and we took off, enjoying our amazing vacation and trying not to think of the unknown future with no promise of jobs or assurance of income. In Helena, Montana, which was one of the post-office addresses we'd given, a telegram was waiting for Hugh, a telegram from Maurice Evans, offering him a role in an all-star production of G. B. Shaw's *Heartbreak House*.

I will always have a special affection for Helena, Montana.

☙ When it became apparent that we were truly moving to New York, there were many smaller decisions to be made. We had seven cats and three dogs. Hugh said to the children, "We will take one cat and one dog." Our seven-year-old son looked at him anxiously. "And one child, Daddy?"

Of course the question came up of where we were going to live in New York with three young children. Jean and Walter Kerr urged us to find a house in Larchmont, where they lived. We were told by various other people that we should find a place in the suburbs for the sake of the children.

One day Hugh said to me, "You don't like the idea of Larchmont."

"No."

"Why not?"

"Jean can go into New York in the evenings to the theatre with Walter. I can't come sit in your dressing room. Jean has a full-time, live-in maid. We don't. You would have one life in the theatre, and the kids and I would have another in the suburbs. They wouldn't have a father and I wouldn't have a husband."

Hugh understood. We never regretted our decision to live in Manhattan, where Hugh could come home for dinner on matinee days, where we could have what I considered a normal family life. Sometimes in the winter when bad snow storms were forecast Hugh would bring another actor home to spend the night, to ensure that he would be able to get to the theatre the next day for the matinee. I thought to myself that I would much rather be the wife giving the slumber party than the wife getting the phone call.

❤ When *Heartbreak House* started rehearsals, Hugh found two rooms in a wonderful old hotel, the Dauphin, now gone to make room for Lincoln Center. There was a beautiful circular living room with large French windows and two pullout couches; a large bedroom with twin beds; a closet kitchenette; an enormous bathroom with mirrored walls—at the turn of the century the Dauphin had been a favorite hotel of opera singers. On Friday afternoons I would pick the children up after school and we would drive to New York for the weekend, the children taking turns with a sleeping bag in the bedroom.

We had a happy several months at the Dauphin. I even managed Christmas dinner with guests, having cooked almost everything at Crosswicks and bringing it down to the city. During the Christmas holidays we started our search for an apartment. The parts of the city that we knew best—the East Eighties, where I had lived until I was twelve, the Village, where we had started our theatre lives—were now out of our financial range. So, it seemed, was every other part of Manhattan. Vacation ended, and we returned to our weekend schedule. One rainy January Saturday the children and I were out apartment hunting, looking at every ad in *The New York Times* which seemed at all possible. But anything we liked was too expensive. Two hundred and fifty dollars a month was, in January of 1960, our outside limit. We were cold and bedraggled and I announced to the children that it was time to go back to the Dauphin to cook dinner for

Hugh between matinee and evening performances. Josephine pointed to an ad: "Luxury apartment, eight rooms, four baths, fourteen closets." No price.

Obviously no point in our even looking at it. But Josephine kept persisting. "Let's just go see it."

"We don't have time."

"But let's just go look, just for fun."

I gave in, and we took the bus and went to look at 924 West End Avenue. And we discovered that it was a rent-controlled building, and while it was hardly a luxury apartment it was big, and it was $128 a month.

We hurried back to the Dauphin to tell Hugh of our find. At first he was disbelieving, but he went with us the next day to look at the apartment, and in a great leap of faith we signed the lease.

We moved in on the first day of February 1960. I was hopeful that not only were we back in my beloved city but that the long series of rejection slips would come to an end. The idea for *A Wrinkle in Time* had come to me during our camping trip, a response to my discovery of Einstein and Planck and the other physicists with their entirely new view of the universe. I had started *Wrinkle* as soon as we got home, and finished it in a white heat. It was very different from my six earlier published books but I loved it, and I hoped that it would mark a turning point. So the continuing rejection slips were especially painful.

Heartbreak House was a wonderful way for Hugh to return to Broadway, working with Maurice Evans, Diana Wynyard, Pamela Browne, Alan Webb. We still have the poster with his name listed among the stars, hanging in the kitchen.

One evening Alan Webb said affectionately, "Hugh, your accent is middle-Atlantic and is fine, though occasionally you come on, announcing, 'I am Hector Hushabye.' Your problem is that you walk like a cowboy. The English actor is tight-assed." True. Hugh always walked with a graceful, long-legged lope.

Once again we were in the precarious world of the theatre, not knowing what would happen when *Heartbreak House* closed, how we were going to be able to pay the rent, the school tuition.

But Hugh got jobs. Television. A couple of movies. He replaced Melvyn Douglas in Gore Vidal's *The Best Man*. He had a minor role in this play, and one night when Douglas was called to California because of his mother's illness, Hugh went on in his place. When the announcement was made that Melvyn Douglas's role would be played by Hugh Franklin there was an audible groan, but few people asked for their money back, and at the end of the evening Hugh received an ovation. So when Douglas left, Hugh moved into the star dressing room and played the role for six months.

❧ We moved back to New York just in time to experience the sixties, the polarization of the country by the Vietnam War, the concomitant passion for peace, the awakening of the women's movement, the fight for civil rights, hippies and flower children. Young men wore long hair; fur coats became taboo; odd or ethnic jewelry was fashionable.

One evening, probably a Sunday, because Hugh was home, we were expecting our younger daughter, Maria, and her current boyfriend. Both were in the middle of their hippie stage. In preparation for their arrival Hugh combed his hair over his forehead, put on jeans and a red turtleneck sweater decorated with several chains of my beads; put an earring in one ear; wore dark glasses; went barefoot. When the doorbell rang he went to open it, expecting Maria and her friend. Instead, it was our son-in-law Alan with a visiting British bishop arriving well before we expected them. Both men were in full clericals, and the bishop had just landed in New York for his first visit to America. I still smile when I think of what he must have felt when the door was opened to him and he saw Hugh. What kind of father-in-law did Alan have? But he took it in stride, with good humor. And Hugh's own face was a study in shock, as he blurted out, on seeing the black suits and dog collars, "But I thought you were Maria and Jim!"

We moved back to the city, I thought, just in time. Our girls were starting to go to school dances and we didn't have to worry about their being driven home from the Regional School by some boy who was drunk or stoned. In the city they walked home or took the bus.

A fashionable East Side church started a Saturday evening dance for young people and our girls were invited. How splendid, we thought, how safe. Josephine went to the first dance; Maria was spending the weekend with a friend. About ten o'clock the phone rang. Hugh answered. It was Josephine. "Daddy, come get me." The party had moved to someone's apartment. Liquor flowed. She went into a bedroom to look for a bathroom and there was a couple in bed. She fled and called home. Hugh took a cab over to the East Side and rescued her. Thank heaven she had the courage to call, "Daddy, come get me!"

&. Our return to the city and the theatre meant that I had to re-examine many of my ideas about marriage. I wanted to be up at night when Hugh came home from the theatre, to fix his supper, to talk. This was important. But we were no longer free to put our children to bed at two in the morning, to let them sleep until we arose. I got up in the morning with the children and fed them their breakfast and saw them off to school. I do not burn the candle well at both ends. I got overtired and ill. So we called a family conference.

I said to the kids, "Your father needs me more in the evening when he comes home from the theatre than you do in the morning before school. We don't like each other very much in the morning, anyhow. I'll get everything ready for you the night before, but you'll have to get yourselves up and dressed and off to school. When you get home in the afternoon I'm yours, all yours. But if you want a living mother this is how we'll have to manage."

It was a difficult decision, but I still think it was the right one. Our children were in on the conference, felt that of course they were old enough to manage on their own. I think it helped them to feel independent. They were seven, ten, and twelve, and competent youngsters, well able to care for themselves in the morning. I had a few pangs of false guilt, largely because I still could not find a publisher for *A Wrinkle in Time*.

❧ In 1962 *A Wrinkle in Time* finally found a home. The book was published by Farrar, Straus and became an immediate, surprise success, and I began to feel that I was finally carrying my own weight. We lived our lives in a slightly chaotic but normal fashion. Between plays Hugh had many times of despondency, going to auditions, to callbacks which came to nothing. But he was an amazingly frequently employed actor as his profession goes.

We both had chosen ways of life where failure and success often intermingled. We learned to understand that failure can be creative, can lead to a maturity which is far better than success. For the human being to live is to live with the open risk of failure.

Being parents is a risk.

A friend said to me, "You and Hugh are not typical parents, you know."

I replied defensively, "We try to be good parents. When the kids came home from school with a request to bake a cake, I baked a cake, and it was terrible, and that's how we came to direct the pageant."

"That's what I mean."

"But we love our kids. We're *good* parents."

"You're marvelous parents. But you aren't typical."

Are anybody's parents typical? Obviously mine weren't, but I loved them dearly and wouldn't have traded them in for anybody else's. I came to know my mother better after my father's death and my move into adulthood and independence than I had before, and she was my friend and confidante all through her long life.

Were Hugh's parents typical? More so, certainly. His father was a respected lawyer. His mother was, to my mind, the perfect housekeeper, and I had to accept, to my rue, that I would never win a merit badge for housekeeping.

Why am I worried about being typical? I don't think I am. One time after I had given a talk to a large library-association annual meeting, one of the librarians asked me, "What do you think you and Hugh do that is best for your children?"

And I answered off the top of my head, "We love each other."

And I'm sure that *is* the best thing we could possibly have given them. But in being lovers, in being parents, we have had to take risks. We have had to be open to crisis.

*   *   *

❧ Hugh is going into renal failure because of the spread of cancer into the ureters. When I say my alphabet of verses as I swim in the morning, it is hard to keep from sobbing; so many of them are intertwined with my life with Hugh.

Charlotte is with us for the weekend, and at night while we are sitting in the four-poster bed sipping cocoa and talking, I say, "Chá, I don't know whether or not Gum is going to make it, but if he doesn't, we've had forty years together, good years, of loving each other, and that's a lot more than many people have."

I know that this is true, but it is hard to accept the spread of the cancer. We learn about the renal failure on the morning of the day when I have promised my friend Dana that I will be with her when she buries her mother's ashes. This gallant woman, full of *joie de vivre,* died of pancreatic cancer in the spring. Dana says, "She's been sitting on Canon Tallis's desk for three months," and it is not meant to be particularly amusing. The ashes of many friends have rested on that capacious desk off and on until the moment comes for burial, either in the Cathedral Columbarium or elsewhere.

Dana has been part of our larger family since she was in high school; she helped take care of my mother during her last summers. When she and Bion were younger they used to have water-pistol fights during the Crosswicks summers (I still have two confiscated water pistols on a shelf in my closet). Now Dana's sons are Bion and Laurie's godsons.

For the burial of Dana's mother's ashes, Bion will drive me to the cemetery in Washington, Connecticut, about half an hour away. It is a tender day, warm, but not hot. There is a gentle breeze. The cemetery is an old one, and peaceful. Dana's mother is to be buried in a wooded corner, beside her own mother. Dana has a basket over her arm, which contains her mother's ashes, and a spray of wildflowers. We are a small group. We each place flowers in the dark hole that has already been dug. Then the urn with the ashes goes in. Then more flowers. Tallis has had typed out a small, traditional burial service which Dana and I take turns reading. The strong words hold us up. We wait until the sexton fills in the hole with dirt. Tamps it down. Replaces the sod. Then we place more flowers on the small grave. Dana's boys are solemn, holding deep inside their grief. We hug, hold hands, touch, reach out for one another.

Then Bion takes me back to the hospital. We do not speak much in the car. There is no need to.

Charlotte is with us again. Bion cooks out, and we sit on the terrace, lingering long past sunset, until the stars come out. Charlotte and I again go up to the four-poster with mugs of cocoa and talk and talk. She will be starting college in New York, staying in our apartment. It is good to know that she will be there, not only to forward the mail, but to keep the apartment warm and lived-in. I have been extraordinarily blessed in being close to my granddaughters for all of their seventeen and eighteen years.

So many people are alone when they have to face the death of the one closest to them. The night we know that the cancer has metastasized, three friends just "happen" to call. "I had you on my mind." I was supposed to go out to dinner that night, but Laurie called and made my excuses. Bion said, "You need to be with your family." I did. Not to moan and wail. Not even to talk much about it all. Just to be there together.

At bedtime Charlotte gives me especially loving hugs. She is now earning some money by helping me with my mail, and she is quick and amazingly professional for one who has just turned seventeen. I am not surprised. I am grateful that my helpers are people to whom I do not mind revealing myself. Whoever works with me, taking dictation, learns all about me.

Right now my vulnerability is on the outside of my skin. Small things bring sobs up to my throat, but thus far only when it has been all right, appropriate, to cry. I have slowly learned a lot about grief, and the right and proper expression of it. Wearing mourning in the old days was not such a bad idea, because it took into visible account the fact of death, which we now try to hide, so that it won't embarrass others. A friend told me that three hours after his wife had been killed in an accident he was told roughly, by his minister, to pull himself together.

We pull ourselves together when we need to. We do the things that have to be done. But we need to give ourselves times and places in which to mourn. This is strength, not weakness. (Yesterday a doctor asked me, standing in the corridor outside Hugh's room, "Do you feel weak or strong?" I replied truthfully, "I feel weak and I feel strong.")

I go to my lonely bed, thinking of Hugh alone in his hospital room, grateful for the nurses who are so good to him. During the night I reach out with my foot through force of habit to touch his sleeping body. And he is not there. Nevertheless, we have been making love during this time in a profound way. He is making love with me in the pressure of his fingers. I am making love when I do simple little bodily services for him. How many times he has taken care of me! And that is intercourse as much as the more usual ways of expressing our sexuality.

Intercourse between two people who are totally committed to each other is a beautiful thing for both. Hugh and I have been true to each other in this day and age of casual affairs, and I'm grateful that we have. I believe that fidelity increases the joy, the actual physical pleasure of lovemaking, and that in a casual affair or a one-night stand, love is not made, only sex. I never want to stop making love.

In Hugh's hospital room, where I spend seven or more hours a day, I am always on the alert toward my husband, even when he is sleeping. My quiet time comes in the evening, when we sit out on the terrace and wait for the stars. Most evenings I go upstairs early, at nine o'clock, to read, to think, to be quiet for a couple of hours. To unwind enough for sleep, which I need if I am to keep up my strength.

Piano time is very slim. I don't get home from the hospital in time to have that treasured hour at the piano before dinner. Writing, too, has been difficult. I have been drafting a novel, but the work has gone slowly. Although I am encouraged to use my little six-pound electronic typewriter in the hospital, I am constantly yearning toward Hugh in inner prayer. Not demanding prayer. Just a small giving of love flowing steadily to him. Most of what I have written this summer is this journal, and it, too, is a form of prayer and a source of strength.

Prayer. What about prayer? A friend wrote to me in genuine concern about Hugh, saying that she didn't understand much about intercessory prayer. I don't, either. Perhaps the greatest saints do. Most of us don't, and that is all right. We don't have to understand to know that prayer is love, and love is never wasted.

Ellis Peters, in *A Morbid Taste for Bones*, one of her delightful medieval whodunits, gives a beautiful description of what I believe to be intercessory prayer: "He prayed as he breathed, forming no words and making no specific requests, only holding in his heart, like broken birds in cupped hands, all those people who were in stress or grief."

And George MacDonald asks, "And why should the good of anyone depend on the prayer of another? I can only reply, Why should my love be powerless to help another?"

I do not believe that our love is powerless, though I am less and less specific in my prayers, simply holding out to God those for whom I am praying.

For a long time I have been praying for my friend whose husband has Alzheimer's disease, visualizing him in the woodworking shop in which he used to take such pride; seeing him make a beautiful table or cabinet, bathed in a lovely light. But he has not gone near the workshop for a long time. He has taken to wandering about the house at night, dangerous in his tottery condition. I am not the only one who has prayed. And his deterioration has accelerated rather than decreased.

Hugh has been surrounded by literally hundreds of prayers, good prayers of light and love.

What happens to all those prayers when not only are they not "answered" but things get far worse than anyone ever anticipated? What about prayer?

We do not know. We will not know in this life. Some prayers are magnificently answered. More than once this has been the case in my own life, glorious miracles of prayer.

But this summer the answers have all been negative. The doctors say, "Everything has gone wrong." One thing after another.

What about prayer?

Surely the prayers have sustained me, are sustaining me. Perhaps there will be unexpected answers to these prayers, answers I may not even be aware of for years. But they are not wasted. They are not lost. I do not know where they have gone, but I believe that God holds them, hand outstretched to receive them like precious pearls.

Nine

What about prayer? To ask is to be human. To know that answers are not going to be given, and yet be willing to continue to ask, is to move into maturity.

Our life in New York, in Hugh's world of theatre, mine of writing, was as full of questions as ever, good questions, deep questions. Only where there are questions can there be acceptance. Perhaps acceptance is the only answer we are given. Our questions of each other, new discoveries, were part of the joy of deepening marriage. Hugh was always an atypical actor, not prone to mirror-gazing, shunning having his picture taken, not seeking publicity, private about his feelings. But he was a professional in the truest sense of the word.

In John Whiting's play, *The Devils*, Hugh played D'Artagnan, and had a gorgeous costume of soft blue velvet, plumed hat, suede boots. After seeing the show one night a friend remarked, "Hugh, when you stand in the spotlight that way, it really brings out the blue of your eyes."

Hugh replied quietly, "I am aware of it."

His deep humility was accompanied by a totally professional understanding of his rich qualities as an actor.

&. Again there were choices to be made, but they were not difficult ones. Most of our friends were serious artists, not wanting to spend evening after evening at the right clubs, being seen. We did go to a nightclub to hear Edith Piaf sing, but we went to see and hear, not to be seen or heard. We developed an aversion to enormous cocktail parties, where a rock band made it necessary for a mob of people to scream at the top of their lungs in order to be heard. Sometimes after the theatre we would go to an opening of a movie, put on at midnight for players. We went to places like Sardi's on occasion, to meet friends, since it was a convenient location. But we did not live, nor want to live, the life of celebrities. Perhaps our years in a small dairy-farm village had made their mark. We were not interested in being seen in the chic places, and our apartment was in a part of the city that was anything but fashionable.

But Hugh worked, and I wrote, and we watched our children grow up, and we were content.

When Hugh opened in Brecht's *Arturo Ui* we expected a Broadway hit and a long run. To everybody's surprise and chagrin, it was panned by the critics, including Walter Kerr, and was to close after the first week. On Saturday I went downtown to have dinner with Hugh between shows. Walter came into the restaurant where we were eating, saw us, walked over to our table, and said, "When can we get together?"

Hugh smiled. "Any time, thanks to you."

Some plays ran longer. Shortly after the untimely demise of

Arturo Ui, Hugh was playing Cardinal Cajetan in John Osgood's *Luther*. He was a good actor and I was proud of him.

Our children left the nest all in the same year, Josephine to marry Alan, Maria to go to college, Bion to boarding school. Hugh moaned, "We're too young to have them all leave home so soon." But it took him only twenty-four hours to adjust. He would ask, half amused, "They were all home last weekend. Why are they coming home this weekend?" It wasn't that we didn't love or want our children, but that we were enjoying being fully together.

Once again Hugh's work with Walter Kerr at Catholic University made a marked difference in his career. His agent called him to ask if he was free to be submitted for a television role in a new soap opera. Hugh told him yes, the part he was playing was going to be finished at the end of the year. The new show was going to be called *All My Children* and the agent wanted to put him up for the part of Dr. Charles Tyler, the doctor who was the head of the hospital and the head of the family. Shortly he called back. "You've got it!"

"Fine," Hugh said, "but why do you sound so surprised?"

"You don't have to audition. They're auditioning everybody else, but they want *you*."

"Fine," Hugh repeated. "Get me as much money as possible."

• The show was to begin on the first of January. In December, ABC gave a party for the new company. I was out of town on a speaking job, so Hugh went alone. During the party a woman came up to him. "Hugh, you probably don't remember me. I was a lowly freshman at Catholic University when you were there in *Hotel Universe* and I've never forgotten you." She remembered him partly because he was superb in the play and partly because his innate courtesy had made him treat the shy young girl with consideration. "I'm Agnes Nixon," she said. Agnes Nixon was the creator of *All My Children*.

Dr. Charles Tyler was rich, privileged, sophisticated. Hugh felt that the character was square, not realizing how much of his own personal warmth and integrity he put into the role.

When we rode the subway, almost inevitably someone would come up to him: "Dr. Tyler, what are *you* doing on the subway?"

One summer evening we were walking along Broadway on our way to see a play. Suddenly we were surrounded by a group of a dozen or so leather-jacketed youths. In today's world this is a bit startling. But what they wanted was Dr. Tyler's signature on dollar bills—and they provided the dollar bills. One young man obligingly turned his back so that Hugh could use his jacket as a desk.

He is recognized everywhere. In airports we are often escorted to first-class lounges because, of course, that is where Dr. Tyler belongs. If I am traveling alone, all I have to do is slip into the conversation that I am married to Dr. Tyler, and then the hostesses give me special service, and want to know all kinds of little details about Dr. Tyler and the show.

Hugh has become, for millions of reasons, a cherished father-figure, a man to be trusted at all times, who is also beautiful to behold, with his white hair, patrician features, and those extraordinary blue eyes.

❧ In the early years of our marriage it was Hugh who was frequently out of town with plays. Now it is my turn to travel, to go off on speaking engagements. But this is far more the normal pattern of our marriage than were the nine years of living daily together at Crosswicks. When we are apart, we are in touch by phone.

"It's snowing," Hugh said one day when I called him the afternoon before I was to fly home from a lecture trip. "In fact, it's blizzarding. I hope things will be better for you when you get home tomorrow."

The next afternoon when I got to the airport the plane was posted as being on time, so I relaxed. Then, just as we should have been boarding, the loudspeaker came on and we were told that because of traffic problems in New York caused by the snow there would be a three-hour delay.

So I arrived in New York long after midnight instead of shortly after nine, and it was indeed a snowy city. When the taxi pulled up in front of our apartment building the street had been plowed, with the result that between the street and the entrance to the building was a six-foot wall of snow.

And there in the lobby, peering anxiously through the glass, was Hugh, who came hurrying out to help me with my bags (always heavy with manuscript), and to give me a much-needed hand over the snowbank. He had called the airport to check on my flight; even so, he had been waiting in the lobby for well over an hour.

When we are together we enjoy each other's company fully. Our routine is simple and pleasurable. In the late afternoon I read the mail, then play the piano for an hour. At seven Hugh comes in to me, clinking a glass, while our dog barks with joy, and we repair to the kitchen to cook dinner and talk over the day's events, in our lives, in the world. At dinner we light the candles and sit in the dining room, often quietly, kything, rather than talking. Then we take the dog for a walk in Riverside Park, come home, and prepare for bed.

Several times Hugh has said, "I love our rut."

So do I.

During Hugh's annual vacation while he was on *All My Children* we traveled together, and this was a special joy. Our favorite vacations were on freighters, but these became more and more difficult for us as the freighter schedules got more and more erratic. Hugh's vacations were set months ahead of time, with no flexibility.

But we always found someplace to go, and after he left the TV show our trips for the USIA were great fun. Perhaps it is because these trips are different from our regular vacations, perhaps it is because we have reached a new phase in our marriage, but we are delighted with each other's presence, delighted with all the new places we see, the people we meet, delighted with a collaboration in our readings that is, in its own way, as much a joyful method of making love as any other.

❧ I look at my husband's beloved body and I am very aware of the mystery of the Word made flesh, his flesh, the flesh of all of us, made potential when that first great Word was spoken that opened the tiny speck from which came all the galaxies, all the solar systems, all of us.

That great beginning was probably a simpler action of the Word than that Word becoming incarnate, the ultimate unfathomable mystery of the Word made flesh.

We cannot explain the incarnation. It is understandably referred to as "the scandal of the particular." It takes every leap of the imagination to accept this amazing impossible gift of the Creator.

I have long felt that the sacrifice of the mystery of the Word made flesh was a far greater sacrifice than the crucifixion. That was bad, yes. Terrible, yes. But it was three hours on the cross, three hours. This summer I have seen in this hospital people dying in agony and by inches, week after week, month after month. Oh, I do not negate the agony on the cross. The abandonment of Jesus by his closest friends. The seeming failure of all for which he had become flesh. It was terrible.

But there are worse deaths. And these deaths make no sense at all unless the mystery of the Word made flesh is present in them too; death makes no sense at all if the God who is in it with us is not in the dying body of the young man down the hall; the people killed, burned, in the most recent air crash; in my husband, in me, our children.

I have come to the hospital this morning just after receiving what my friend Tallis calls "the holy mysteries," bread and wine which are bread and wine but are also more than bread and wine, since the bread and wine, like the stars, like the snow, like all of us, is made of the original substance of creation, that which Jesus put on as human flesh. It is by these holy mysteries that I live, that I am sustained.

• We ate out on the terrace again last night; there may not be many more nights this late summer when it will be warm enough for us to eat outdoors, and that, too, was a holy mystery. We live surrounded by mystery.

Carrying my babies was a marvelous mystery, lives growing unseen except by the slow swelling of my belly. Death is an even greater mystery. I don't want to be afraid to ask the big questions that have no answers. The God I cry out to in anguish or joy can neither be proved nor disproved. The hope I have that death is not the end of all our questions can neither be proved nor disproved. I have a great deal left to learn, and I believe that God's love will give me continuing opportunities for learning. And in this learning we will become truer to God's image in us.

It is said that the subconscious mind cannot conceive of its own extinction. Most of the time the conscious mind cannot, either. We know that we are going to die, but most of the time we don't believe it.

There is a theory that people have to finish working out relations until love is perfected. How that is going to be brought about is in the hands of the Maker, and I am willing to leave it in the realm of mystery, in the design of the *misterium tremendum et fascinans*. Do lovers meet again after death? That, too, is held in the mystery of the Word made flesh. It is a reminder that faith is not for the things we can prove, but for the things we cannot prove; that it is not for the conceivable but for the mysterious.

Each day in my alphabet of prayer I recite, in faltering Spanish, words attributed to John of the Cross; even the saints, perhaps particularly the saints, grapple with the questions with which we all fumble.

No me mueve, Señor, para quererte
El cielo que nos tienes prometido.
Ni me mueve el infierno tan temido
Para por eso no ofenderte.

Tú me mueves, mi Dios; muéveme el verte
Clavado en una cruz y escarnecido;
Muéveme el ver tu cuerpo tan herido,
Muévenme tus afrentas y tu muerte.

Muéveme al fin tu amor, y de tal manera
Que aunque no hubiero cielo, yo te amara,
Y aunque no hubiero infierno, te temiera.

Ya no tienes que darme porque te quiera,
Que aunque lo que espero no esperara,
Lo mismo que te quiero te quisiera.

My friend Dana translated it for me thus:

I am not moved, my God, to love you
By the heaven you have promised me.
Neither does hell, so feared, move me
To keep me from offending you.

You move me, Lord, I am moved seeing you
Scoffed at and nailed on a cross.
I am moved seeing your body so wounded.
Your injuries and your death move me.

It is your love that moves me, and in such a way
That even though there were no heaven,
    I would love you,
And even though there were no hell,
    I would fear you.

You do not have to give me anything
    so that I love you,
For even if I didn't hope for what I hope,
As I love you now, so would I love you.

I have always taken these last lines to mean: Even if what I
hope for is not what is going to be, no matter what, I would love
the one who made me.

These are not new thoughts for me, nor for most of us, but

they are made more poignant by the events of this summer. We still do not know the results of the bone and liver scans, the CAT scan. The doctors still have not made up their minds which route to take. Do nothing more than continue the radiation as a palliative to slow down the kidney failure? Or take the risk of surgery? It would be a big risk—but worth it, if the cancer has not spread into the bones or liver.

The doctors know how I feel. I want Hugh to live, dearly, dearly do I want him to live, if he can be returned to real life. But I do not want dying (rather than living) to be prolonged for him. Over and over we have promised each other that we will not let this happen.

Most crucified people took three days to die on the cross; Jesus was given death in six hours.

The medical profession is at a time of crisis because of the amazing instruments of modern medicine. They save lives. But they also prolong dying horrendously. The Church is at a time of crisis, too, seeming to fall into the same dilemma as the scientists, that of attempting to prolong the life of the body even when the person is gone. God did not do this to Jesus. Shouldn't we have learned something from that?

Ten

*T*ouch. The Mystery of the Word Made Flesh. I sit on the edge of the hospital bed and hold Hugh's hand. I have to touch him very carefully, very gently, in order not to awaken the pain, and I long to put my arms around him, to have him put his arms around me. I want us to be able to hold each other. But right now the holding can be only that of the spirit.

Hugh has worked through a lot these past months, all the appropriate steps of fear and anger and rejection and acceptance and into a warm and loving and gallant response to all the indignities. My gratitude to the nurses who help him keep as much modesty and human dignity as possible is unbounded. But neither they nor I can take away from him the inevitable loneliness of gravely serious illness.

Some of the nurses themselves are going through their own passions. One has a son with leukemia who is waiting for a bone-marrow transplant. Another has just watched her mother die. Because I am present in the hospital for so many hours each day I have the opportunity to come to know some of these people who hide their own hurts as they work on healing for others.

* * *

❧ It is the fourth of September. Once again this evening I read that anguished cry, "My God, my God, why have you forsaken me!" The cry of the Word made flesh, the total mystery of the human being.

Big decisions have been made today. Lung and liver and bone scan, CAT scans show that perhaps the platinum chemotherapy was not wasted. The cancer, aggressive though it is, is contained within the pelvic area. The radiation treatments will be continued to shrink the malignancy where it has spread into the ureters, but this is barely palliative. Hugh is going to die of renal failure if something is not done at once.

There can be no waiting until he is strong enough. Next week the big surgery will be performed. It is big surgery at the best of times, the remaking of all the body's internal plumbing, and this is not the best of times. We all know—Hugh, the doctors—that it is a risk, and we are all agreed that it is a risk worth taking.

When Herb talked with Hugh about it this morning, and asked him what he felt, Hugh said, "I'm all for it."

It is Hugh's own decision. None of us could make it for him. He has made it, firmly, alone with his doctor.

We have not talked a great deal about it verbally, Hugh and I. But we have talked enough. Better, we have kythed, that silent communion which deepens between two people as they live together for many years. When our fingers are touching, we are communing as well as communicating.

When I touch the mystery of his flesh, "Word of God, our flesh that fashioned with the fire of life impassioned," I am touching ultimate mystery.

* * *

❧ There is a mystery to all love. Why does this one man so move me? Why does this small corner of our planet make me feel that I am home?

We live in an uprooted society. During the long years of my father's dying my mother was uprooted. When he died she returned to her roots, to a Southern town where almost everybody was kin, where her childhood friends still lived. I used to love to read Louisa May Alcott's *Eight Cousins*, her story of a wonderfully warm and variegated New England family, and Mother told me that her Southern family was very much like that. Almost all of her friends and playmates were cousins.

One of the best things about this present, difficult summer is that I have felt rooted. I am in the house that Hugh and I have loved for forty years. During the brief times that Hugh has been at home, rather than in the hospital, I have dug in the garden; sometimes he has been up to sitting in a garden chair watching as I have planted, weeded, plunging my hands into the rich earth. Amazingly, the vegetables have flourished, despite the inevitable neglect.

The forty years of our marriage are deeply rooted in Crosswicks. In a chest of drawers in the attic are children's clothes which are still passed around as needed, especially the beautiful little smocked dresses my mother gave to my daughters. Even the pots and pans are part of the rootedness. This double boiler was given to me early in our marriage by my beloved Mrs. O, who loved me without qualification until she died in her mid-nineties, and whose love I believe is still with me. This old-fashioned rice cooker came from my grandmother's kitchen in the South. This rebound Bible belonged to my great-grandmother Madeleine L'Engle, after whom I am named; her hands turned and marked the pages I read; her tears spotted them.

When I walk the dogs at night I walk on land that has been familiar under my feet for forty years. It may be because I was a city child, born and raised on the asphalt island of Manhattan, that the actual feel of grass, of earth, is something of which I am acutely, joyfully aware. Above me the stars are part of the root-edness, stars which are patterned in the sky in a particular way in this corner of the planet.

I am blessed in being rooted with my family, with Bion and Laurie making their own roots in this house which is well over two hundred years old. Charlotte is with us frequently. Maria and John are coming this weekend, with John's parents staying with the babies so that the young parents can have one night of sleeping straight through the night; and so that they can have some time with Hugh. Josephine calls her father in the hospital every evening, and is ready to take a plane East at any moment. This kind of love dwindles the miles.

Food is part of the rootedness, food and water. Our water comes from our own artesian well. We know, as much as can be known nowadays, what we are drinking. Much of what we eat comes from the garden, and the evening meal is a special part of the rootedness, when we linger at the table, lighting candles or oil lamps as the sky darkens. We have consciously eaten well this summer, knowing that this quiet time of relaxation and pleasure is important, for we are weary, the body/spirit worn by all that has been happening. We eat the first young corn, which Hugh planted and now cannot eat. Fix a platter of sliced tomatoes and green peppers, sprinkled with basil and chives.

At night I go upstairs to a bed that is generations older than my marriage, a high four-poster bed in which Hugh and I have made love, and in which others before us have made love for more than two centuries. There is a good feeling to the bed, as there is to the house. Life has been lived in it fully. There are no residual auras of anger or frustration, but a sense of the ordinary problems of living worked out with love and laughter.

Each time Hugh has had to go back to the hospital it has been an uprooting wrench for him. He yearns for the familiarity of his own bed, sheets, blankets, his own windows, with their own view. His own bathroom, with his toothbrush in the china holder. Being uprooted is one of the hardest parts of hospitalization. I leave him in the evening and go home and it is as though my roots are restored.

We talk with him about the new projects in and about the house and land. We tell him that the corn he planted just before this illness struck him is ripe for eating. But we cannot take away his uprootedness.

When he sleeps, he looks like an El Greco saint, translucent, beautiful. But this is a beauty that makes me ache as I look at it. I want the old rootedness, and I don't know if that will ever be given again.

Tonight it is suddenly chilly and damp, and Bion, Laurie, and I eat in front of the big fireplace in the living room. How often we have sat there, eaten there, in comfortable companionableness. I remember Hugh saying that looking at the flames in the fireplace gives one somewhat the same sense of peace as looking at the ocean waves rolling in to the shore.

A friend came by this afternoon to visit with Hugh and remarked that his unhappiness with the world of the yuppies is that their rootedness is only in money—money not as that which makes it possible for us to buy bread and milk and a roof over the head, but as a symbol of transitory vanities. Was he being too harsh? I'm not sure.

But it reminded me that my own rootedness must be expressed

in and through symbol and sacrament or it is not rootedness at all. When I dig in the garden it is God's earth, given us to care for and nourish. It is all undergirded by the understanding of what "a goodly heritage" I have, and this gift is one I must honor in all that I do and all that I am. But right now the pattern is clouded with chaos, as still one more thing and still one more thing goes wrong for Hugh.

It is decided to give him hyperalimentation to prepare him for surgery. This means that a triple lumen must be surgically placed in his upper chest. In this way he will be able to be given much greater nourishment than by the smaller IVs. He is still not able to eat well enough to do without this extra strengthening. The radiation treatment is causing the expected nausea, which of course makes eating all the more painful.

A general surgeon is called. He tries to put a needle in the left side of the chest and is hindered by Hugh's old broken collarbone. Even on the right side it takes two tries before the X-ray shows that all is in place. It is a tiring and uncomfortable procedure.

Late in the afternoon the surgeon returns to the room to tell us that as he was trying to get into the left side of the chest, the slightly enlarged left lung was nicked, and Hugh has a small pneumothorax—a partially collapsed left lung. The surgeon says there is only a small amount of air in the lung, and he thinks it will absorb by itself. Laurie had warned us of this possibility; it is evidently something which cannot always be avoided in this new procedure.

But it is one more thing, another echthroid attack on a body which has already endured one indignity after another.

*   *   *

This morning when I come into Hugh's hospital room the oncologist is saying, "Hugh, it seems that anything that can go wrong is still going wrong." This morning's X-ray shows that the pneumothorax has increased by forty percent, rather than decreased. This is Saturday. Surgery is scheduled for Tuesday. There is not time to wait for the lung to reinflate on its own.

The young general surgeon comes in. Amazingly, I am allowed to stay in the room, to hold Hugh's hand. It is explained that a tube will have to be put between the ribs and into the chest so that the invasive air will be sucked out. The tube will have to stay in place until after the surgery.

The surgeon prepares, donning surgical gloves. A nurse is with him to hand him the local anesthetic, sterile fluid, ultimately the scalpel. I stand at the head of the bed where I can clasp Hugh's hand and he can hold hard when the pain is bad. He is given several shots of local anesthetic. Then the surgeon takes a small scalpel and makes an incision a little over an inch long just above the ribs. Then he tells Hugh that what is coming next is going to hurt, and he will hear a great whoosh of air. The surgeon puts his fingers in the incision, feeling for the right place; then the tube is thrust in and air does indeed whoosh out and Hugh almost screams with pain. But the tube is in, and then the incision is sewn up. There is a plastic tank hung at the side of the bed. "You will sound like an aquarium," the surgeon says, and so Hugh does. He is exhausted and in pain.

For the first time since this last hospitalization he complains, whispering, "This is really one thing too many . . ." It is, it is. I am grateful only that I was allowed to be with him. I hope it helped to have my hand to hold, my presence to assure him of my love. It was probably easier for me to be there with Hugh than to have to wait out in the hall. But I, too, am exhausted; my body feels as though it has taken some of Hugh's trauma.

Hugh is in bad pain. "What has happened to my voice?" His beautiful, strong voice is a hoarse whisper. The nurse thinks it is from the shock of the procedure. A pill for pain has been prescribed, but it is apparent that the ulcerated esophagus is too sore and too strictured for him to be able to swallow a pill and keep it down. The charge nurse and I confer and she calls the oncologist, who prescribes a hypodermic, which Hugh is finally given, so that he can relax enough to nap. He looks like death.

He wakes and whispers, "This begins to be funny," and indeed an accumulation of tragedy begins to break down into comedy.

But this is too much, too much. I feel that Hugh is being pursued by the Eumenides. Or that we ought to call a priest to come in with bell, book, and candle to exorcise him. What echthroid devil is breaking through all the prayers of love and light?

I remember Luci Shaw saying to me when my eye was injured, "Madeleine, I think this is demonic interference." Surely we are naïve if we do not believe that there are fallen angels, echthroi, nephilim, or by whatever name they are called, who are attacking the light. I must hold firm to the faith that the light can be neither comprehended by them nor extinguished.

On the phone last night I told Maria how much better her father looked, that she needn't be afraid to see him. Now I am afraid that she and John are going to be terribly shocked, and this weekend at Crosswicks was planned for their relaxation.

They are already there, helping Bion and Laurie make apple cider. It is good for the young parents to have a day when they don't have to watch their toddler every second; to have a night when they don't have to get up every few hours to feed the baby, who is two months old today. They, too, are exhausted. They will come down around six o'clock to pick me up and visit, but Hugh is in too much pain and too worn out to be able to enjoy it.

Last night Josephine called again from San Francisco, wanting to come East for the surgery, but I was dubious; she has just been here, less than two weeks ago, for her father's seventieth birthday; she is an entire continent away. But after we had hung up I called back. "Please come. I need you." She had already bought her ticket for the next day.

Gretchen, one of our godchildren, comes in this afternoon. Her own father, our long-term friend who had first shown us Crosswicks and assured us the well-built old house was sound under all the disrepair, has to have back surgery next week. While Hugh is sleeping, Gretchen and I sit and talk, and she almost undoes me by saying that Hugh and I are her role models for marriage. Gretchen lived with us during her junior year at college, so she is not talking out of thin air.

Two other godchildren are coming tomorrow. One of the doctors remarked that Hugh seems surprised he is so much loved.

The pain shot has let Hugh's body relax enough so that he is sleeping quietly. The newspaper is on his bed table. A few days ago there was another terrible plane disaster. Yesterday another ghastly hijacking, with "at least seventeen dead." The eight-month-old granddaughter of a friend has died of a sudden high fever. What is happening? The echthroi are stalking.

The punctured lung is statistically beyond bounds. In the morning I call my friend Tallis in New York. "I have a strange but completely serious request. Can you do an exorcism in absentia?" We talk a little about all that has been happening. I say, "Whenever people do terrible and violent things, more powers of darkness are unleashed." Terrible and violent things have been happening in the world around us, and he agrees with me. "I will do what I can," he promises.

He is an Episcopal priest, a canon of a great cathedral, a totally orthodox Christian theologian, orthodox enough to see nothing strange in my request. If we are all made of the stuff of stars, and if the stuff of stars is the stuff of Jesus, then distance should make no difference to the efficacy of prayer, prayer that the powers of darkness will leave my husband so that God's light of love can bathe him, body, mind, spirit. And it does.

The next morning when Maria and John drive me down to the hospital, Hugh is better, does not look like death as he did the night before. His own vibrant voice has returned. I am grateful beyond words that they will be able to return to New Jersey with a better picture of Hugh in their mind's eye. We hug goodbye.

🐚 At Trinity Episcopal Church in Torrington, where I go for the Wednesday morning communion service with my friend Gillian, there is a brand-new rector. He has just come: I see him on the Wednesday after his first Sunday. It turns out (oh, wonderfully small world!) that he is a friend of Josephine and Alan's, that he knows the family. Immediately he goes to the hospital to see Hugh, and there is instant rapport between the two men. Faithfully Joe comes daily, often in the evening after visiting hours are over and I have gone home, and the two men talk and talk. Hugh is from Oklahoma, Joe from Kansas; they have many bonds in common; Joe's father was a doctor, Hugh's a lawyer; Hugh can talk to Joe as he cannot to those of us who are too close to him.

The church has been good to us this summer. The Congregational minister visits faithfully; on Sundays, prays for Hugh with the congregation, most sensitively and lovingly.

Now that September has come and school and autumn activities have started, after twenty-five years I am once again singing with the choir, my heart eased by the warmth of my reception and the loveliness of the music.

My daughter Josephine arrives. It is more good even than I knew it would be to see her again. We talk together at night in the four-poster bed, that bed where there have been so many deep and loving conversations. We talk too late, but it is worth it. The day before the surgery we spend with Hugh at the hospital. He is in acute pain from the chest tube, but he manages to smile, to joke.

The next morning I come down to the hospital early with Laurie. I am dressed in an outfit Hugh particularly likes, and he remarks on it. Smiles for the nurses. An orderly comes in with a stretcher. I look at the nurses, who have been taking such good care of him. "It's going to hurt him a lot to be moved onto the stretcher . . ."

"Hold on," one of them says. "I'll call the OR."

In a few moments the phone rings and she answers it and says, smiling, "You're going up in your bed."

"We don't do this for everybody," the orderly says. "You're getting very special treatment."

It is obvious that they are pleased. I am encouraged to walk along beside the bed to the elevator. To kiss my husband.

He has gone up to the OR half an hour before schedule, so Bion and Josephine, stepping out of the elevator, have just missed him. We go on home. Bion goes to work. Josephine and I go up to the library to go over some business that can't wait.

Hugh was taken up to surgery at nine-thirty. It is a four-hour procedure. "They won't have started exactly at ten," we tell ourselves. "We can't possibly hear before two."

Two. Two-thirty. Three. We look at each other. Work a little harder. Three-thirty. Finally the phone rings. It is the urologist. Hugh is in the recovery room. The surgery was even more complicated than anticipated, took nearly six hours rather than four, but Hugh has come through it. By early evening he will be in the intensive care unit and we will be able to visit with him for a few minutes.

Herb thinks he has removed all of the cancer out of the ureters, so that the kidneys can function again. There is some nodal involvement. He is not at all sure what they will do about that. Radiation? More chemotherapy, despite Hugh's intolerance to it? Right now, no such decisions will be made. The important thing is to get Hugh through the post-op period.

We visit him briefly in ICU. He is hooked up to a respirator, which is doing his breathing for him. He is attached to tubes and monitors. He is aware enough of our presence to smile with those vivid blue eyes, to give a small pressure of his fingers, but that is all. We go on home.

Sit on the terrace quietly for dinner. Early in the day Bion made one of his famous spaghetti sauces so we wouldn't have to do more than put together a salad from the garden. The stars come out while we sit there, clear, bright. A young moon is setting.

As evening darkens, the Milky Way sweeps across the sky.

Hugh made it through the surgery. We were not at all sure that he would, and he did.

"I am cautiously optimistic," Herb says.

Nevertheless, the future is still very uncertain.

But I am not called to project into this still-unknown future; rather, I am called to be fully in the moment. I am sitting with three people I love, and we are surrounded with loveliness. The breeze is gentle. The autumn insects are singing. There is an incredible reality to this moment because of my intense awareness of it, my intense awareness that I still have a husband. This is how we should be all the time and seldom are, as we get caught in the overbusyness of life. But now, at this moment, I am caught in the wonder of the *misterium tremendum et fascinans*.

Eleven

---

*I*t does not matter that we cannot fathom this mystery. The only real problem comes when we think that we have. We glimpse it in poetry and song, in revelation and marvel, but it is not to be greedily or arrogantly grasped.

Lady Julian of Norwich wrote: "He said not 'Thou shalt not be troubled, thou shalt not be travailed, thou shalt not be distressed,' but He said, 'Thou shalt not be overcome.' It is God's will that we take heed to these words, that we may be ever mighty in faithful trust in weal and woe."

Faithful in the small things as well as the great. Last night an early frost threatened. We harvested what we could in the garden, which has borne plentifully despite the fact that there has been little time to weed or take care of what we have planted. Then we covered the still-ripening plants with ancient shower curtains and sheets to protect them, something we have to do every early autumn on cold nights when there is not enough wind to blow the frost away. On our windy hill we are often spared the early frosts that hit the valleys.

Autumn? Internally I am still waiting for summer.

But Labor Day has come and gone. The trees and fields are

still green and sometimes I don't see the color that is painting the trees. Wednesday is my ecumenical day: Gillian comes for me in the morning to take me to the eucharist at Trinity Church. Afterwards Joe is ready to hug me, to tell me some of the things he and Hugh have talked about. In the evening a friend comes to pick me up for choir practice in the Congregational Church. But my life is largely focused on Hugh's hospital room.

Right now we must wait. The urologist is pleased with the results of surgery, pleased with Hugh's recovery, repeats that he is cautiously optimistic. Every day brings improvement. But we do not know whether or not the sharks are still waiting to attack.

They are.

September is moving toward its close. The spindlewood tree as I look out my bedroom window this morning is flame. I swim my ritual laps, have breakfast, do a few chores, and then Bion drives me to the hospital.

The morning nurse and I are chatting as she bathes Hugh, and suddenly she sees blood, calls me, and we both look; his wound has opened and is spilling out blood. The nurses on the floor are competent, compassionate, quick. The wound is held together and pressure applied. But it continues to rip apart, until two rosy coils of intestine slip out. An emergency call is put in to the urologist. Meanwhile, the nurses keep the open wound and the intestines moist with sterile saline solution. They are calm and reassuring.

"Are you all right?" I am asked.

Yes, I am all right. I have faith in these nurses, these nourishers.

Herb comes and Hugh is quickly taken up to the OR. This is going to require general anesthesia, which means that another chest tube will have to be put in to protect the fragile lung. The entire wound will have to be reopened and resutured.

After a long, cold hour Herb calls to say that Hugh is awake and alert, and will be down soon.

I don't want this to have happened. I don't want my beloved to have had one setback after another, to go on suffering. I don't know what is going to happen next.

But I am beyond anger, I am in a dark place where I simply exist in the pain of this moment.

Before he went up to surgery Hugh whispered, "I don't know why, but this has made me teary."

"Darling, I know why. It's too much. It's not fair." It's beyond not being fair. It's statistically excessive.

🙞 But on Saturday he seems to be doing well, to be again on the road to recovery. Bion and Laurie and I talked about the possibility of renting a hospital bed when Hugh comes home so that he can be on the screened porch with its lovely views, so that we will not have to worry about stairs.

I am urged not to cancel a long-made plan for a brief trip to New York on Tuesday. It's the publication date of my new book, *Many Waters*, and my publishers have planned a dinner party. It would be a very brief trip, a meeting of the Authors Guild executive council and the dinner, and I am more than willing to admit that I need a break. We are no longer thinking in terms of a complete cure as we were earlier in the summer, but there is still the hope that the surgery was successful enough so that Hugh will have some good months, if not years, as long as nothing else goes wrong in the post-operative weeks.

Joe, the Episcopal priest who has so quickly become a friend, plans to bring in books and papers and spend most of the day with Hugh. Friends will drop by, and of course Bion and Laurie will be there.

On Sunday morning I go for an early swim, walk the dogs, and set out to church for nine o'clock choir rehearsal. Church is at ten. At the time of the "Concerns of the Church," we pray for Hugh. He is wrapped in prayer.

One of the soloists is the granddaughter of the soprano who was the chief soloist in the days when I directed the choir. The soprano is an alto now, still singing. I feel a wonderful sense of continuity.

As soon as we have sung the final Amen I hurry out of my choir robe and out of the church, eager to get down to the hospital.

And I see Bion and Laurie waiting for me.

While I was in church Michael, the oncologist, called. Hugh is not doing well. He has vomited blood. He is having a hard time breathing. It may be a pulmonary embolism, which Michael cannot treat because Hugh is already bleeding. Or it could be pneumonia, which is treatable. He told them not to get me out of church, but to be there waiting for me to get me down to the hospital as quickly as possible.

I feel cold and stunned on the drive. We hurry up to his floor. Hugh has on the oxygen face cone and is breathing with difficulty. I stand and hold his hand until Laurie moves a chair so that I can sit and still hold his hand. The nurse who has been taking care of him this morning whispers, "I'm sorry." She cares.

After a while I tell Bion and Laurie to go on home. I spend the day sitting by Hugh's bed, mostly just holding his hand. One of the nurses asks, "No typewriter today?"

"Not today." Even when Hugh is sleeping my focus is entirely on him.

Then, in the afternoon, he rallies. His breathing eases. He asks for the paper. Michael comes in. Says he does not know why this episode has happened. Says he will be back later in the evening.

It seems to me that the splitting of the wound, the extra surgery and anesthesia are enough trauma to have produced this. Who knows?

Two of our godchildren, Bion's and Laurie's age, had planned to come for a visit, have dinner, and then drive on back to New York. They go to the house first, and Bion and Laurie alert them to what is going on. They will be married in less than a month. Their emotions are close to the surface and this is a blow to them.

About seven-thirty, when the nurses are working on Hugh's IVs, I see them standing in the doorway and go out to them, and am wrapped in love and hugs. It is compassion that has undone me all day. One of the morning nurses came to me, saying, "You need a hug," and put her arms around me. Another made a great effort to get me a cup of hot coffee. When the afternoon shift came on, a lovely young nurse who has taken wonderful care of Hugh said, "Oh, it isn't fair! It shouldn't have happened to him!" And she, too, put her arms around me. It was hard not to spill tears. Well, they did spill, but then I got them back under control, not wanting Hugh to see me and be frightened—not for himself, but for me.

"How should we pray?" our godson asks.

"Pray for whatever is best for Hugh."

They go in to him, talk to him about their forthcoming wedding. Even now he pulls himself up to joke lovingly with them, tells them not to expect him to make it to the wedding, and then advises them not to use the hospital caterer.

I go home with them, reluctantly. I want to stay, but I know that I must have food and rest. We do not know how long this vigil is going to last.

Bion has called his sisters, Hugh's sister. The doctors, the nurses, all of us, thought that this was it, that Hugh was going to die this morning. And he didn't.

We have a quiet dinner, the five of us, and then the lovers drive back to the city.

Is this a reprieve? Oh, let it be a reprieve.

&❧ Monday morning, early, Laurie calls the hospital. The nurses report that Hugh is better, breathing more easily. She will look in on him as she makes her morning rounds. At nine, as soon as the switchboard opens, I call my publishers to tell them that I can't leave Hugh right now, and could we please reschedule the party? Of course.

How blessed we are in our godchildren. Gretchen, living over an hour away in Hartford, drives all the way over to Goshen to take me to the hospital, since this is a day when Bion has to be at the university by eight. Gretchen is married now, busy with teenaged children. We talk, deeply, about God and love and marriage, in the same totally real way we have been able to talk all these years.

Hugh is better, is rallying. I spend the day with him. When he naps I pull out my little Typestar and write. He is not up to reading. But his breathing is easier. They have taken off the big face mask, which he said made him feel claustrophobic, and he has only the two small nose prongs for oxygen. I come home for dinner and bed. Wake around three-thirty and pad down to the kitchen to make hot milk with nutmeg. Read for a while. Sleep again. Wake. Sleep.

Tuesday morning. The first official day of autumn. The day I was supposed to go to New York. Crosswicks is wrapped in fog. Bion is able to drive me down to the hospital and drops of slow rain trickle down the windshield like tears.

As soon as we see Hugh, we know that things are not good. He has been throwing up, watery green bile. He is breathing with difficulty. His voice is weak, but almost the first thing he says is, "I thought you were going to New York."

"I'm not about to leave till you're feeling stronger."

"But the party—"

"We can reschedule it."

His concern keeps surfacing. "What about your Authors Guild meeting?"

"The vice president will take it for me. He'll be fine. We had a long conference call yesterday afternoon while you were sleeping. Don't worry."

Laurie is already in the hospital doing morning rounds. She comes in and Bion and I look at her anxiously. The nurse is ready to bathe Hugh, so we go out into the corridor. Laurie goes to the nurses' station for Hugh's chart. Checks the results of tests. Michael has written, "Situation deteriorating." I did not need to see it written down to know, yet it is still shocking.

We come back to the room and tell Bion to go home. He has work to do. Laurie sits with me until she has to leave for a meeting.

Hugh whispers, "I never was so glad to see anybody as you this afternoon."

"It's still morning, darling. I'm going to be with you all day."

We hold hands until he falls asleep.

Is he dying? Today? I don't know. Modern medicine has made it less and less easy for us to predict the imminence of death.

Joe comes in. Hugh is too weak to talk, but he manages a smile, both on his lips and in those great blue eyes, so often remarked on by the nurses. He slips into sleep, and Joe and I talk quietly. I am so grateful that these two good men have found each other.

Joe says to me, "Hugh is the victim of modern medicine."

Hugh lies there, the two small prongs of oxygen in his nose. The chest tube is still in place, the chest tube that was the result of the effort to give him hyperalimentation. His belly is sewn up so that the wound cannot come apart.

But what was the alternative? The treatment Hugh was given has cured people. The older methods, such as radiation, were successful only in postponing death, not in killing this kind of cancer. Had he not been given the platinum, what kind of death would he have suffered? I don't know the answer to these questions. But because we have new ways of treating disease, we use them.

Hugh has had no intractable pain. The worst has been from the chest tube, which the surgeon admits is painful, but the pain has never been beyond relief. If we had to make all the choices again, what would we choose?

And I remember Ed saying, "I have thought about this long and prayerfully, and it is what I would do for my father." So we had to do what there was to do.

At the end of a long letter Scott Peck wrote: "On an intellectual level, Elisabeth Kübler-Ross's stages of death and dying come to mind, and it seems to me, at least in retrospect, that Hugh had reached stage five (which very few are fortunate enough to do) which is a stage of light and, basically, resurrection. It was a real privilege to witness. Obviously, your marriage had something to do with that extraordinary phenomenon. Although I had heard some of the details from Lily, I cannot imagine what the next six weeks were like for you. But I gather, rightly or wrongly, that they were strangely peaceful."

In a strange way, yes.

Daily, Hugh and I express what we feel, simply by saying and saying again, "I love you." Hugh and I have been saying it off and on for forty years. It comes off the lips of our children, our godchildren. It is all that needs to be said. I told Gretchen yesterday that Hugh and I have no unfinished business. There are no dangling strings left to be tied. I don't want him to leave me, but even more I don't want any more useless suffering for him. He is so gallant, so gallant, even today managing to smile for the nurses. For me.

I look at him, beautiful as an El Greco saint, for that is still the analogy that keeps coming to my mind. When I get home I look at a snapshot of the two of us together, Hugh's face alert and alive. I observe and contemplate this child of love, made of the same stuff as galaxies and stars. And I know that the only meaning is love.

🙚 Laurie comes to pick me up and take me home after her evening rounds. On the drive back I tell her that I want to be with Hugh all the way to the end; I want to be with him when he dies.

Laurie explains that it is not that easy. If he starts to go, there will be a Code Blue, nurses and doctors will come rushing, I'd be thrust out of the room.

"No."

He'd be put on a respirator, isolated in ICU.

"No."

After the big bladder surgery, the first night that Hugh was in ICU he was on a respirator, a tube down his throat so that he couldn't talk. There was a gastronasal tube, heart monitor, IVs; his hands were loosely tied to the sides of the bed. The next day, when the respirator was gone and he was able to talk, he told us how terribly frustrated he had been that he could not make the nurses understand that he was deaf and couldn't hear.

I don't want that for him. In his own room I am able to be with him all day. In ICU it's basically five minutes on the hour, though they are good about bending the rules. But they could not be good enough.

Laurie then explains to me that the only way to avoid this is to have NO CODE written into his chart.

At dinner that evening I talk with her and Bion about it. I tell them that Hugh and I have promised each other, not once, but several times, that we would never allow this prolongation of dying to happen. I tell them that I want to honor my promise. They look at me, nod in agreement. I telephone my daughters, telling them, too, about the promise. They, too, agree.

❧ This morning NO CODE is written into his chart.

Actually, he is a little better this morning. But I am glad that the decision has been made. Both Michael and Herb are in complete accord.

One of the nurses tells me that this is what was done with her husband. The doctor simply told her that this was how it was going to be handled; no "heroic measures" to prolong dying. About my age now, she was twenty-five years younger when her husband was dying, and she said she fell apart, but as she looks back on it, she wouldn't have had it any other way.

"Today," I said, "the doctor would not be allowed to make

that decision, no matter how much he felt it needed to be made."

She agreed. "You have to do it. But it's a hard decision."

"I love him."

I think of Lady Julian. "Wouldst thou witten thy Lord's meaning in these things? Wit it well. Love was his meaning."

On Thursday, Hugh is very weak. He is dehydrated, despite the IVs, and his mind wanders. He goes back to his childhood in Oklahoma. I know that this is often a sign that death is approaching. Sometimes he thinks he has to learn lines, go to rehearsal. Sometimes his mind is completely clear.

It is a beautiful day, and Thursday is Laurie's afternoon off; she and Bion go for a climb. Autumn is unusually early. The trees are turning their brilliant reds and golds. Leaves are falling.

They pick me up a little before seven. I have promised to take them to a small local restaurant for dinner. None of us feels like cooking, cleaning up. I tell them that I am terribly anxious about Hugh.

We kiss him good night, tell him that we love him. Bion says, "We're taking Mother out to dinner."

Hugh says, "Have a good dinner," manages to smile for us, is with us.

As soon as we get home after the meal Laurie calls the nurses' station. Hugh is sleeping quietly.

I open a small mail-order package, and there are some socks I ordered for Hugh when it still seemed likely that he would be with us for Christmas, and this undoes me utterly. We realize with terrible finality that Hugh is not going to come home, and we hold each other and weep together.

Was it two days ago that Herb and I, in the corridor outside Hugh's room, talked about the possibility of his coming home, of having a few months of quality life, of enjoying the new addition and all that we have done while he has been in the hospital?

We sob brokenly, sharing our grief.

&. In the morning I have just finished my pre-breakfast swim when the phone rings. Laurie comes out. The hospital has called. I hurry to get dressed. As we are leaving, Michael calls. I say that we're on our way.

When we get to the hospital the elevators are on upper floors, so I run up the stairs. Michael is in the room. Hugh has vomited, and ingested some of the fluid. His breathing is strained, and he has on the oxygen face mask. He is not conscious.

I hold his hand. Touch. Look at Michael and tell him I know he has done everything possible.

He nods. "One domino fell over after another."

Bion and Laurie come in. We are all touching Hugh's hands, arms, shoulders, touching. I am not sure when Michael leaves. Herb comes in, presses my shoulder. "We're with you."

Does Hugh understand that he is being touched, loved? Is there enough awareness in him for that?

At ten o'clock I call Josephine, call Maria, tell them that their father is going. Still touching my husband, I hold the phone in my other hand and say goodbye to my daughters.

Hold Hugh's hand. Touching. Stroking. Suddenly light green fluid washes over my right hand. I hold Hugh's head up, push the lever to raise the head of the bed with my other hand.

Hear Laurie say, "This is it."

Hugh stops breathing. I am holding his head, his shoulder. Laurie goes out to call one of the nurses, who comes in with her stethoscope. There is no pulse, no heartbeat.

I continue to hold him. To touch. Several nurses come in, whisper, "I'm sorry," They cry with us.

When Michael comes in to pronounce death, I say, "It is hard to let go beloved flesh."

He nods.

Hugh is still warm.

Twelve

We go home. Josephine calls to say that they have been able to make a plane reservation, and she and Alan will leave at once with nine-year-old Edward and will arrive at Bradley late that evening. Charlotte calls to say that she and Léna will take the bus to Cornwall Bridge, as close as public transportation comes to us, and will arrive a little after seven. Maria and John will come the next day, with John's parents again staying with the babies. There are many phone calls to make. I have called Hugh's sister from the hospital. We make a list, dividing the calls.

And our phone starts to ring.

There has been no sentimentality, no false or guilt-ridden love. We have been able to avoid the death-prolonging so often forced on people by technocracy, which makes death far more difficult by what appears to be a vicious type of sentimentality. Thank God I was able to make the choice of NO CODE, to keep my promise to my husband. This time I had to do it for Hugh. He was too ill and too disoriented to make it for himself. But he made the choice with me, long ago.

We have called Joe, who has meant so much to Hugh, and to whom Hugh has meant so much. We call Charlie, the Congregational minister who has been so faithful. We decide to have the funeral on Sunday at three o'clock in the afternoon, the best time for those who will be able to drive up from New York.

The day is a blur. We receive a call telling us that the women of the church will take care of the reception at Crosswicks after the funeral—what Hugh would have wanted to have called his "party." My community swings into action, into support. The funeral baked meats start to pour in. We are surrounded by love.

I wanted this resolved, and I know it was time, but it is still a terrible wrench, an amputation. Hugh had already had a dreadful four months, and I didn't want him to go on suffering, but I wasn't quite prepared for how devastated I would be.

I discover that tears are very hard on contact lenses. One would think that since the lenses rest on the eye's tears, crying would be good for them, but it isn't. Too much salt, I suppose. And I can't wear glasses, am totally dependent on the lenses to see.

I take them off and lie down, try to rest. My feet and legs start to cramp. Despite the daily swim I have been unusually sedentary, sitting by Hugh's hospital bed day after day. And I feel cold, a deep, inner cold. It is not the terrible cold of hell, but simply the cold of shock following a great loss. I get up and into a hot tub and warm up and then am able to rest.

My granddaughters arrive and there is much loving, much hugging. We eat a quiet dinner out on the screened porch. This is their first encounter with the death of someone dear and close to them.

I am in bed, waiting, when Alan and Josephine and Edward arrive at eleven-thirty. Although it is late and we are all exhausted, both psychically and physically, of course we sit and talk. I ask Alan to do a Requiem Mass, and he immediately says he will celebrate it on Monday in Joe's Trinity Church. And Tallis, who has been so close to us for so many years, will celebrate a Requiem for Hugh at the Cathedral when I can get down to the city. Celebrate, yes. We will celebrate Hugh's life. I do not go in for what are called "white funerals," with Easter music, as though Good Friday had never happened. The kind of celebration I can be part of is one of great joy for Hugh's life, and of great and deep grief at the same time.

I'm alternately calm and carrying on with the things that need to be done, and overwhelmed. It's the small things that do it, such as seeing the shaving brush we bought for Hugh when we were in Hong Kong—only last May.

We've all been housecleaning like mad. John vacuums everywhere. Charlotte is in the middle of cleaning the fridge, and has polished the silver.

The three older grandchildren, Léna, Charlotte, Edward, are going to read the lessons at the funeral Sunday afternoon.

Sunday. The summer is over. Autumn is fully here. Hugh has what in the theatre is called "a full house" for his funeral. I am overwhelmed at the people who come—not only the Goshen community, but many from New York, and from the *All My Children* company. Our goddaughter Cornelia, who had flown out to her parents' in Seattle on Thursday, flew back to New York on Saturday in order to be able to drive up to Crosswicks on Sunday, and will go back to Seattle on Monday. The response of love is overwhelming.

The service is simple and dignified and beautiful, with the two ministers who have been so faithful during Hugh's long illness taking it together. The grandchildren have rehearsed and rehearsed the Scripture readings; their grandfather would be proud of them. The hymns are "A Mighty Fortress Is Our God," which we sang at my mother's funeral, and "Joyful, joyful, we adore thee," which was Hugh's favorite, and doesn't quite make me break down. Hugh had asked to be cremated, and the most difficult part is when Charlie picks up the box of Hugh's ashes and carries them out at the end of the service.

We don't take count, but well over a hundred people come back to the house, and the Goshen churchwomen take care of everything—beautifully. It is a nice enough day so that we can spread out onto the terrace. Ernie and the boys, home from college for the weekend, the boys for whom we gave the cookout the day of the evening we knew that Hugh's cancer had spread, go way above and beyond the call of duty and come on both Saturday and Sunday to clean up what is still a mess of wood and equipment, outdoors and in, and finish the screened porch so that all the food can be set up there, and basically the party— yes, that's what it is, what Hugh wanted—is on the porch and the terrace.

Oh, we had hoped that Hugh could come home, could be with us long enough to enjoy the porch. But it was not to be. He had worked through all the anger and confusion during the middle hospitalization and right after. During his final hospitalization, his last six weeks, all his sweetness and humor were to the fore. My love died a very good death.

✸ Monday morning at ten is the eucharist at Trinity Church. Again, it is simple, dignified. At the intercessions I offer thanks for the nurses, who were so wonderful with Hugh. And during the greetings at the Passing of the Peace I am deeply moved to see one of the nurses there, on her day off. She says, "I want you to know I speak for all of the nurses when I say it was an honor to take care of him."

After the service we ask people to come home for lunch— fridge and freezer are still full of all the goodies we have been given, from casseroles to roasts. Bion and Laurie and I detour to the hospital to take the nurses some of the cakes and cookies, as a small token of thanks, and they are caring and pleased to see us. They truly loved Hugh.

❧ Now I am setting out into the unknown. It will take me a long while to work through the grief. There are no shortcuts; it has to be gone through.

Slowly the house empties. Maria and John must go back to their babies. Josephine and Alan and their three leave. My friend Pat comes from Florida to be with me for a week, that same Pat with whom I have shared life and death and love and sorrow and tears and laughter since we were both gawky teenagers. The evening after she arrives she gets a phone call from her youngest son, and his wife has just had a baby boy. They had come from Fairfield to be at Hugh's funeral just three days before the baby was born. The next Sunday Pat and I drive over for a visit. I am ultimately given the baby to hold, and since it is in my arms that this charming five-day-old creature falls asleep, I hold him longest, slowly rocking, holding new life.

The phone continues to ring, many of our beloved godchildren who live too far away to have come to us, sobbing into the phone. One of my love-children wails, "But what happened to our prayers? Didn't they do any good? Were they all wasted?"

"No, no," I reassure, "never wasted. Of course they did good. Hugh never had intractable pain. His last weeks were a beautiful witness of sweetness and courage and humor."

"But they didn't work!"

"Of course they worked. Not the way you wanted them to, but your godfather died a good and holy death."

A friend calls, reaching out via the phone, and tells me that she has just come from running an Elderhostel weekend. She had this group of older men and women go outdoors to try to find a symbol in nature that would be meaningful for them. One woman came to her with an empty nutshell, saying, "My husband died a year ago, and I am like this nutshell, empty."

I know that my nutshell is not empty. It is full of memory, memory of all my life, memory of the forty years of Hugh's and my marriage. It is the foundation of this memory which helps me keep on with my work, and that is what Hugh would want me to do. I go to a university campus to give a lecture, and it is hard, because the last two times I was there I was with Hugh, giving readings with him. But this year's students do not know the past. The lecture goes well. I am exhausted, but the step has been taken.

Someone tells me a story of a bishop who lost his wife and child in a tragic accident. And he said to his people, "I have been all the way to the bottom. And it is solid."

Yes.

A couple of years ago a friend called me from her hospital bed, demanding, "Madeleine, do you believe everything that you have written in your books?"

I said *yes* then. It is still *yes* today.

But grief still has to be worked through. It is like walking through water. Sometimes there are little waves lapping about my feet. Sometimes there is an enormous breaker that knocks me down. Sometimes there is a sudden and fierce squall. But I know that many waters cannot quench love, neither can the floods drown it.

We are not good about admitting grief, we Americans. It is embarrassing. We turn away, afraid that it might happen to us. But it is part of life, and it has to be gone through.

I think of the character Mado (modeled after my great-grandmother Madeleine L'Engle) in *The Other Side of the Sun*. She lost home, husband, children, and she made the journey through the burning flames of the sun. It cannot be gone around; it has to be gone through. But my grief is a clean grief. I loved my husband for forty years. That love has not and does not end, and that is good.

I think again of that evening after I had come home from a speaking trip and said to Hugh, "Wherever I go, you are with me." Surely that is still true.

Does a marriage end with the death of one of the partners? In a way, yes. I made my promises to Hugh "till death us do part," and that has happened. But the marriage contract is not the love that builds up over many years, and which never ends, as the circle of our wedding band never ends. Hugh will always be part of me, go with me wherever I go, and that is good because, despite our faults and flaws and failures, what we gave each other was good. I am who I am because of our years together, freed by his acceptance and love of me.

Bion and Laurie are at Crosswicks. That is indeed a blessing. And so are my granddaughters a blessing. Charlotte and one of her college friends are living with me in the apartment in New York. Léna is just up the street in a Barnard dorm and comes to us frequently. One evening I want to have some friends in for dinner. So do my granddaughters. So we have a combination dinner party, and to my amazement and joy the girls love the chronological mix.

Every other week or so, Charlotte will say, "Gran, it's time we had another party." We have anywhere from a dozen to two dozen guests. I do the cooking, the girls do the cleaning up. We usually represent six decades. Last Sunday evening the youngest was six months old; there were two ten-year-olds, half a dozen teenagers, several in their twenties, thirties, forties. I'm not sure about the fifties. And then all the way up to me, in my late sixties. Conversation is general, with no sense of chronological alienation, and this is how it should be. Some evenings there are performers among the guests, and then we have music. Chronology swirled for me as Léna and Charlotte belted out some of the songs from Broadway musicals their mother had sung when she was their age.

One evening I sit in my quiet place in my room, to read evening prayer, write in my journal, have some quiet *be*ing time. The sky over the Hudson is heavy with snow. Léna and Charlotte are downtown at a Chelsea coffeehouse with friends; they will have to take the subway home. I write in my journal that the more people I love, the more vulnerable I am.

Vulnerable—the moment we are born we are vulnerable, and a human infant is the most vulnerable of all creatures. The very nature of our being leads us to risk.

When I married I opened myself to the possibility of great joy and great pain and I have known both. Hugh's death is like an amputation. But would I be willing to protect myself by having rejected marriage? By having rejected love? No. I wouldn't have missed a minute of it, not any of it.

The girls and I have acquired two kittens. They are vying for my attention. One of them starts diligently grooming me. The other bats at my pen. This is less an invitation to play than an announcement that it is time for bed. Even with the kittens I am vulnerable as they curl up trustingly beside me and hum their contented purrs.

❧ I get to Crosswicks whenever I can, to relax in the deep rhythm of the house, filled with the living of over two centuries. That richness of experience permeates the rooms, life lived to the utmost, birth and death, joy and grief, laughter and tears.

It is good to be part of the laughter as we sit around the table by candlelight. A wood fire both lightens and warms the room. None of the fullness of life in this old house is lost. The forty years of Hugh's and my marriage is part of the rhythm.

Music I heard with you was more than music, and bread I broke with you was more than bread.

Yes. And always will be.

Also from Lion Publishing

MEET THE AUSTINS
The first in the Austin family series

Madeleine L'Engle

'It makes the grapefruit come out wrong, to have five
children, instead of four.'
   It's not only the grapefruit which comes out wrong
when recently orphaned Maggy Hamilton comes to
stay. The Austin family are easy-going and full of
fun, but before long they all find their patience and
humour being put to the test.
   Seen through the eyes of twelve-year-old Vicky,
the events following Maggy's arrival are often
surprising, sometimes sad, and occasionally hilarious.
But they're never dull.

ISBN 0 7459 1385 7

THE MOON BY NIGHT
The second in the Austin family series

Madeleine L'Engle

'Maybe nothing would ever be as comforting and
secure as it used to be . . . but it was going to be
exciting.'
  Just how exciting is something Vicky Austin might
never have guessed. The Austins' camping trip
across America soon turns into an adventure, as they
have to face floods, an earthquake and even wild
bears. But, for teenage Vicky, the most important
event is her encounter with the elusive Zachary Grey.

ISBN 0 7459 1384 9

Also from Lion Publishing

A RING OF ENDLESS LIGHT
The third in the Austin family series

Madeleine L'Engle

'. . . this was the first time I'd been involved in this
part of death, this strange, terrible saying goodbye to
someone you've loved.'
    The death of a family friend isn't the only tragedy
of the summer, and Vicky Austin sometimes
wonders if she'll ever be happy again. But that's
before she is befriended by Adam Eddington and his
remarkable dolphins.

ISBN 0 7459 1383 0

A selection of top titles from LION PUBLISHING

MEET THE AUSTINS	Madeleine L'Engle	£1.95 ☐
THE MOON BY NIGHT	Madeleine L'Engle	£2.25 ☐
A RING OF ENDLESS LIGHT	Madeleine L'Engle	£2.25 ☐
FACE TO FACE WITH CANCER	Marion Stroud	£3.95 ☐
WHEN SOMEONE YOU LOVE IS DYING	Ruth Kopp	£4.95 ☐
COPING WITH DEPRESSION	Myra Chave-Jones	£1.95 ☐
LISTENING TO YOUR FEELINGS	Myra Chave-Jones	£3.95 ☐
THE STRESS MYTH	Richard Ecker	£3.95 ☐
THE LONG ROAD HOME	Wendy Green	£1.95 ☐
YOUR MARRIAGE	Peg and Lee Rankin	£2.50 ☐
GETTING MARRIED IN CHURCH	Mary Batchelor	£1.95 ☐

All Lion paperbacks are available from your local bookshop or newsagent, or can be ordered direct from the address below. Just tick the titles you want and fill in the form.

Name (Block letters)
_____

Address
_____

_____

Write to Lion Publishing, Cash Sales Department, PO Box 11, Falmouth, Cornwall TR10 9EN, England.

Please enclose a cheque or postal order to the value of the cover price plus:

UK: 60p for the first book, 25p for the second book and 14p for each additional book ordered to a maximum charge of £1.90.

OVERSEAS: £1.25 for the first book plus 25p per copy for each additional book.

BFPO: 60p for the first book, 22p for the second book plus 14p per copy for the next seven books, thereafter 8p per book.

Lion Publishing reserves the right to show on covers and charge new retail prices which may differ from those previously advertised in the text or elsewhere, and to increase postal rates in accordance with the Post Office.